UNCONSCIOUS

STUDIES IN
PHILOSOPHICAL PSYCHOLOGY

Edited by
R. F. HOLLAND

The UNCONSCIOUS

A Conceptual Analysis

by

A. C. MacINTYRE

HUMANITIES PRESS
ATLANTIC HIGHLANDS N.J.

First published in the United States of America 1958
by Humanities Press Inc.
171 *First Avenue*
Atlantic Highlands
New Jersey 07716

© *by Alasdair C. MacIntyre,* 1958

Second impression 1962
Third impression 1965
Fourth impression 1967
Reprinted and first published as a paperback 1976

ISBN 0 391 00336 4

Printed in Great Britain

CONTENTS

INTRODUCTORY AND
BIBLIOGRAPHICAL NOTE

TOO many philosophical writers on psycho-analysis have attempted to solve all · their problems at one attempt by saying what *the* status of psychoanalytic propositions is. It is therefore perhaps worth stressing at the outset what I have reiterated in the essay that I am here concerned only with one central concept of psychoanalysis, although its linkages with other concepts make it impossible to isolate the discussion from a discussion of some kindred topics. For I recognize that psychoanalytic theory is so complex and various that when one has disentangled the strands which I have dealt with here one is only at the beginning. I ought to say that the gap between theory and therapy which I point to in this essay seems to me already to be largely overcome in the metapsychologies of Melanie Klein and Fairbairn. But to enlarge upon this would be to write another essay.

The works to which reference is chiefly made are:

I. Psychoanalytic writings:
    Ernest Jones. *Sigmund Freud: Life and Work.* Vols. I and II. (Hogarth Press).
    Sigmund Freud. *The Interpretation of Dreams* (Hogarth Press).
    ——*Collected Papers: Vol IV: Paper V. Repres-*

sion. Paper VI. The Unconscious. (Hogarth Press).

On therapy, apart from case-histories the most illuminating writings which I know are:

Sigmund Freud. *Collected Papers: Vol II: Paper XXVI. Observations on 'Wild' Psycho-Analysis. Papers XXXI–XXXIV. Further Recommendations in the Technique of Psycho-Analysis.* (Hogarth Press).

James Strachey. *The Nature of the Therapeutic Action of Psychoanalysis.* International Journal of Psycho-Analysis, 1934, Vol. XV.

II. Philosophical writings:

Basic to the contemporary discussion are Professor Gilbert Ryle's *The Concept of Mind* and Ludwig Wittgenstein's *Philosophical Investigations.* The important papers are:

'The Logical Status of Psycho-Analysis' by Stephen Toulmin.

'Psycho-Analytic Explanation' by Antony Flew.

'Cause, Cure and Motive' by Richard Peters.

These all appeared in the journal *Analysis* and were printed in *Philosophy and Analysis*, edited by Margaret Macdonald (Blackwell).

'Intentions' by J. A. Passmore. Aristotelian Soc. Supp. Vol. XXIX, 1955.

'Motives' by D. J. McCracken. Aristotelian Soc. Supp. Vol. XXVI, 1952.

'Mind As Feeling' by J. Anderson. Australasian Journal of Philosophy and Psychology. Vol. XII, 2.

'Motives and The Unconscious' by A. G. N. Flew in *The Foundations of Science and the Concepts of Psychology and Psychoanalysis* (Minnesota Studies in the Philosophy of Science).

'Freud's Theory' by Richard Peters. *British Journal for the Philosophy of Science,* Vol. VII, No. 25, 1956.

This last paper is the best example known to me of a statement of Freudian theory clarified by logical analysis. It deserves a place under both my bibliographical headings.

I would like finally to express my indebtedness to Mr. David Hamlyn from whose unpublished writing on this subject I have profited; to Mr. Roy Holland and Professor D. M. Emmet whose criticism of my manuscript has greatly improved it; and to numerous colleagues, too many to mention by name, from whom I have learnt.

University of Leeds   A. C. MacIntyre
October 1957

CHAPTER ONE

PROLEGOMENA

O F the concepts fashioned by recent and contemporary psychology none has so impressed itself upon the public mind as the concept of the unconscious. No doubt there are a variety of reasons for this, but one stands out. It is that this essentially simple notion seems able to relate a far wider range of disparate human phenomena and to subsume the wildly abnormal and the tediously normal activities of human beings under the same headings far more easily than any other explanatory concept advanced so far. Seems able, rather than is able, for here I am speaking of claims made and impressions received rather than of facts established. The importance of this can only be brought out by putting these claims in the context of the aspirations of psychologists. Psychology is today a field that presents a striking contrast. On the one hand there is an enormous quantity of solid experimental and clinical investigation going on in a piece-meal way. A tremendous variety of correlations between different aspects of human action and passion are being established. But most of this work goes on with only the

sketchiest theoretical background to it. At the same
time psychologists are extremely self-conscious
about the need for developing comprehensive theories. They are apt to compare the present state of
their science with that of physics immediately before
Newton. The physicists had then established a great
many low-level correlations between different
physical phenomena, had observed an immense
number of different regular sequences such as those
incorporated in Kepler's laws of planetary motion.
But it needed the theoretical genius of a Newton to
explain the whole range of phenomena by means of a
few simple concepts which could be given mathe-
matical expression, such as the concept of gravita-
tional attraction. Pre-Newtonian physicists had
however the advantage over contemporary experimental psychologists that they did not know they
were waiting for Newton. By contrast the hankering
of psychologists after a comprehensive theory leads
to their surrounding what is in fact a spectacle of
industry and achievement that merits nothing but
intellectual respect by a haze of aspiration which re-
sembles nothing so much as waiting for a theoretical
Godot.

This, however, is only one side of the picture.
There are also those who believe that psychology
does not need to await its Newton, not because, as
might be maintained, the desire for a Newtonian
transformation of psychology is itself misconceived,
but because psychology has already found its Newton. In the sharpest contrast with the often unre-
lated and fragmentary work of the experimentalists

stand the complex and intricate theoretical struc-
tures erected by Freud and Jung. Here the difficulty
is the opposite to that in the experimental field. So
closely inter-related are their various theoretical
concepts that it is sometimes difficult to be certain
how the observations adduced as evidence for the
system and the key-concepts of the system are in
fact related. It is therefore very much to the point to
enquire into the justification of such concepts and
the present essay is precisely concerned to enquire
how the concept of the unconscious is in fact to be
justified.

The question is not, in the form at least in which it
is being put here, an empirical one. It is not a question of how good the evidence is for the existence of
an unconscious mind but a question of what kind
of evidence is relevant to claims about the unconscious, what kind of reasons are appropriate in the
justification of such claims. We are concerned not
with the correctness of the observations of Freud and
his psychoanalytic successors but with the nature of
their theoretical interpretation. What is offered
here is a logical analysis of a theoretical concept,
and any conclusions that may be reached will be
conclusions of the kind that can appropriately be
drawn from such an analysis. With the success or
otherwise of psychoanalysis as a therapeutic method
I am not concerned here. But this is not to say that
the point of this inquiry is completely divorced from
questions of therapeutic success. For if psychoanalysis had not achieved notable successes in healing mental disorder, an inquiry such as this would

be deprived of any importance it may possess. We do not waste time analysing the theoretical concepts of astrology.

One of the most obvious features of the concept of the unconscious raises another difficulty about the direction of this inquiry. It is that there is no one clear-cut concept of 'the' unconscious, as there is one clear-cut concept of the electron. Freud has one concept, Jung has another, the neo-Freudians seem to have a third. But priorities here are quite clear. Not only does Freud's conception of the unconscious merit analysis on its own account, but as a matter of historical fact other and later conceptions spring from it (at least so far as attempts at a conception at once scientific and detailed are concerned). So that a case for going straight to Freud's writings is plain. But which of Freud's writings? If it were possible to examine a few selected texts in which the kernel of Freud's doctrine was laid bare, this would be the ideal method. But in fact those writings of Freud in which the concept of the unconscious is treated most fully are the theoretical essays and in them very little attention is often paid directly to the clinical material which the concept is intended to illuminate. So one is forced, for a complete picture, to go to case histories and theoretical essays as well, of course, as to the more systematic works.

One last preliminary point: it is sometimes claimed that a thorough and successful psychoanalysis is a necessary prerequisite for understanding psychoanalytic doctrine and that a failure to accept portions of the doctrine is symptomatic of unconscious resistances which prevent one from seeing its truth. The present writer must admit at the outset that he lacks this prerequisite, if such it be; but a simple logical distinction will perhaps serve to draw the teeth from the objection that I should therefore not embark on this enterprise at all. The causes which lead a man to hold a set of beliefs are always to be distinguished from the reasons which can be adduced in support of those beliefs. I shall support my contention with reasons whose validity will therefore be independent of the truth of any causal account of how I came to advance these contentions. If psychoanalysts think that I misrepresent Freud, or draw wrong conclusions about his achievement, this will I hope be an occasion for them to clarify the authentic psychoanalytic doctrine so that it may not be so misunderstood in future. But it is perhaps worth saying at the outset that I should not even want to begin on an essay like this were I not persuaded of Freud's essential and unassailable greatness.

———————◆———————

CHAPTER TWO

FREUD'S ACCOUNT OF THE UNCONSCIOUS

MY aim in this section is to present Freud's discovery of the unconscious in his own terms,
commenting only insofar as it is necessary to bring
out ambiguities in the course of his exposition. 'It is
generally held,' writes Dr. Ernest Jones, 'that
Freud's greatest contribution to science . . . was his
conception of an *unconscious mind.*' But Dr. Jones
at once goes on to note what Freud himself asserted
at his seventieth birthday celebrations. 'The poets
and philosophers before me discovered the unconscious. What I discovered was the scientific method
by which the unconscious can be studied.' The reference to 'poets and philosophers' is not merely a vague
allusion. So far as poetry is concerned we have only
to remember the themes of German Romanticism;
and of the philosophers in question the most notable
presumably is the philosophical psychologist, Herbart. The resemblances between Freud's conception
of the unconscious and Herbart's are striking but the
crucial difference between them appears in the
grounds they give for adopting their respective

6

concepts. For Herbart unconscious mental activity is a simple inference from conscious states. 'Science knows more than what is actually experienced only because what is experienced is unthinkable without examining what is concealed. One must be able to recognize from what is experienced the traces of what is stirring and acting 'behind the curtains!' Freud himself sometimes speaks like this, but the considerations that led him to adopt the concept of unconscious mental activity were of course far more profound. For, taken by themselves, the workaday phenomena of consciousness—whatever we may mean by that none too happy word—are not such that we can validly infer from their nature and occurrence the existence of such unconscious activity. William James dealt faithfully in *The Principles of Psychology* with those who wish to postulate an unconscious mind on account of such occurrences as temporary forgetfulness or the fact that the solution to a problem may spring to mind effortlessly some time after our preliminary brooding on the problem had been abandoned for want of success. For it may be that this is just how things happen in consciousness: happenings such as these only seem to stand in need of explanation if we are able to assume that we ought to have expected them to happen otherwise. And we have no inherent right to make this assumption. Suppose, however, that we concede the right to look for a background to conscious mental activity, a background that exerts a causal influence on consciousness. It is still not the case that we need to postulate the unconscious to

B

provide such a background. For we are well aware of the existence of just such a background in the brain and the central nervous system. The realm, at once obvious and legitimate, in which to seek for causal explanations of conscious mental activity is that of the neurologist. This is where Freud himself started to look for such explanations. It was indeed precisely on account of the weaknesses and failures of the neurological explanations provided by his teachers and his contemporaries that he proceeded to advance an alternative type of explanation.

This is not the place, even were I qualified to do so, to provide a detailed historical account of Freud's progress in the years in which his theories took on definite shape, that is the years immediately before and after the turn of the century. In any case Dr. Jones's biography has made any such account superfluous. But what emerges from Dr. Jones's narrative, and it emerges all the more clearly because of the extraordinary mastery of the source material which that narrative betrays, is that there is no plain and tidy tale to tell. Freud moved towards his central conceptions from a number of directions simultaneously. His criticisms of hypnotic treatment and of neuro-surgery, his self-analysis, his detailed work on dreams, such early cases as that of 'Dora': all these provide possible starting points for discussion. At the same time to concentrate over-much on any one of these may be dangerous. For Freud is not over-careful about terminology and, although if his early papers are read together, the central claims that he is making become quite clear, the emphases on detail are very different in different places. These two considerations taken together make precise exegesis a complicated matter. Although I shall stress the development of Freud's theories as a departure from a neurological standpoint, it will I hope be clear that there are a number of other ways in which this development could be described, all of them equally legitimate.

The failure to cure mental disorders by physical methods—and the inability to provide any explanation of even the sporadic successes which these methods then enjoyed (an inability, be it noted, which larger successes with such methods have left untouched)—were particularly notable in cases of hysteria. Investigation of hysterical paralyses showed that the area paralysed corresponded not to any objectively definable anatomical or physiological area, but the patient's subjective usually somewhat, and occasionally largely, erroneous notions. This suggested inexorably a control of the paralysis by mental and not physiological factors. That the patient was unaware of this provides the justification for seeking the postulated mental activity somewhere other than in consciousness. In a paper written by Freud and Breuer what was to become Freud's doctrine is stated aphoristically in the dictum: 'hysterical patients suffer mainly from reminiscences'. To elucidate what is being said here two other concepts which play a key role for Freud must be introduced, namely the concept of a traumatic event and that of abreaction. A trauma is an occurrence of an emotionally important kind where either the occurrence itself is so painful or the circumstances of its occurrence are such that the emotion aroused cannot find expression. Abreaction is the release of pent up emotion, of which Freud had experience in patients treated by hypnotic suggestion. This release is associated with the recalling of memories which in normal consciousness could not be recalled. Freud and Breuer relate traumatic events and abreaction to the aetiology of hysteria by means of a third concept which Freud made his own. This is the concept of repression. A trauma leads to repressed emotion which, until and unless it is abreacted, causes neurotic symptoms, such as those manifested in hysterical paralyses. And the cure of the symptoms can only be brought about by finding some outlet for the repressed emotion other than the development of the symptoms, that is by finding some method of abreaction. The candidates offered as possible occasions of trauma are fright, shame and physical pain. In the context of this particular paper by Freud and Breuer these concepts are associated with several theses which Freud either did not mention again or later positively disowned, but in themselves they provided a permanent framework for his theory. The trauma occasions a memory which, burdened with the emotion that was aroused by the trauma itself but could not at that time find expression, is repressed and reappears in the form of neurotic symptoms which are a defence of the personality against the repressed emotion and which can be removed by finding a means of releasing the emotion. The decisive point in the development of the concept of the unconscious has arrived. The unconscious is the realm of repressed memories and emotions. The introduction of the concept of the unconscious in this way is conditioned in two aspects which presumably derive only from Freud and not at all from Breuer, since they seem to be attributable to the influence of Herbart and perhaps to that of Freud's own teacher in philosophy, Brentano. The first is that this picture of repressed memory is framed in terms of a Herbartian 'psychology of ideas'. The word 'idea' has a sense here not dissimilar to that which it has in British empiricist philosophy and especially in Locke. It is a discrete unit of mental life, associated in various ways with other such units. Freud conceives of the memory of the trauma as just such an 'idea'. Such an idea can be laden with feeling to greater or lesser degree, and to release the feeling we have to bring the idea to consciousness. Even when Freud does not use the word, this conception of 'ideas' dominates the development of the notion of unconscious contents. Secondly, this kind of account in which ideas are almost transformed into a kind of entity lends itself to spatial metaphors. In many of his early papers Freud was both reacting against and critical of attempts to localize in physiological or, more specifically, neurological terms the causal mechanisms of the psychoneuroses. But the way he talks about memories, for example, is conducive to a new kind of localization, to talk about the mind as a place or a number of places in which ideas move about. How Freud comes to give a mainly topographical account of the mind so that the unconscious is conceived of as a sort of place is a theme that will have to be developed further. But before this can be done adequately we must examine the way in which Freud's conceptual innovations were related to his invention of new therapeutic techniques.

The treatment of mental disorder by psychoanalysis was so revolutionary a therapeutic measure that to stress here how Freud's insight grew out of his practical experience of hypnotic methods might minimize his originality to a quite misleading extent. But Freud's own descriptions of the analytic process are all coloured by the fact that at the time that he was developing it he was also developing his own theoretical concepts; so that he rarely, if ever, gives a purely descriptive account of psychoanalysis. And thus neither a historical account nor a paraphrase of one of Freud's descriptions will give us the type of account that we need, one namely that does not already employ the theoretical concepts to describe the method but shows how the method as practised led Freud on to adopt the theoretical concepts. I shall therefore attempt to give a bare non-theoretical descriptive account of psychoanalytic treatment. Such an account will necessarily be of the form 'And then so-and-so happens, and then . . .' rather than 'And therefore . . .' For in a non-theoretical account nothing will be explained: explanation is the function of the theoretical concepts. And of course a method of treatment wherein nothing is explained would be an odd method to adopt (although scarcely odder than the physical methods of contemporary psychiatry), capable only of pragmatic justification. Freud never offered nor conceived of psychoanalysis as such a method and therefore never gave us such a non-theoretical description of the process. My account will thus be a highly artificial abstraction from what Freud actually says.

In psychoanalysis the patient talks, saying whatever it occurs to him to say. In thus talking he will in fact tend to dwell on some subjects rather than on others, he will pass by some topics and continually return to others. When he dwells on some topic or when he displays great emotion the analyst will tend to suggest an interpretation to him of what he is saying. The more the analysis progresses the more the patient will pass from talk about adult life to talk about childhood and incidents that had apparently been forgotten will be recalled. This recalling will be accompanied by an emotional release. Such emotional release will in turn be followed by a mitigation of the neurotic symptoms which were the occasion of undertaking psychoanalytic treatment. This skeleton account must now be expanded and as it is expanded we shall see how the theoretical concepts fall into place. The patient passes from talk about adult life to talk about childhood *because* resistance to accepting the analyst's interpretation of the repressed memory of the traumatic event is overcome. Here 'resistance', 'repressed' and 'traumatic' are all theoretical rather than descriptive terms. Let us begin by elucidating 'traumatic'. Freud originally agreed with Breuer in seeing the trauma as simply the event which brings on the neurotic symptoms. But he very quickly came to see the onset of the neurosis not as the first event in a causal chain but as the terminus of a cause-and-effect relation going back to early childhood. To say that an event is traumatic therefore is now no longer simply to say that it is the kind of an event that universally precedes a neurosis. The evidence that an event is traumatic is that, after an initial resistance to referring to it, it is talked about in the course of analysis with a good deal of emotion. The very use of the word therefore has introduced an explanation, has connected, for example, childhood incident and adult symptom. One can in principle always observe any event that can be called traumatic, but to say that an event is traumatic is to go beyond anything that can be observed. It is to assert a connection—itself unobservable like all theoretical connections—between two observables.

In explaining the meaning of 'traumatic' reference has already had to be made to resistance, and, like 'traumatic', 'resistance' is not a descriptive but an explanatory, a theory-laden expression. The patient does not remember certain experiences of childhood; when in his own free associations he approaches them he is thrown into a state of some agitation or betrays emotion in some other way; when the analyst suggests that he is avoiding reference to them he repudiates this interpretation of his behaviour with some force: from all this the analyst will infer that the patient is resisting the recall to mind of some memory. But the patient is *ex hypo-*

thesi unconscious of the fact of resistance. To say that the patient is resisting such an act of recollection is to explain as well as to describe his behaviour. But the same is the case with 'repression'. Freud sometimes suggests that the fact that a memory has been repressed is an inference from the fact of resistance. At other times he speaks of it as though it was an inference from the mere inability to remember. But, like resistance, repression is necessarily unconscious. The patient *ex hypothesi* cannot remember repressing. The analyst cannot observe repression. He explains observed behaviour by the hypothesis of a repressed memory.

It is thus clear that Freud's psychoanalytic technique no less than his doctrine of the mind depend on certain key theoretical concepts which can only be understood in terms of each other. This mutual interdependence of concepts in the closely woven fabric of a general theory is nothing new in the history of science. The interrelation of 'mass', 'velocity' and 'force' in Newtonian mechanics springs to mind immediately. But clearly, a comprehensive theory whose concepts are thus interwoven stands all the more in need of justification as a whole. And the whole concept of 'the unconscious' stands or falls with this general theory. For the variety of concepts which we have already met all interlock in the conception of the Unconscious as the realm of mental activity of which we are not consciously aware. We have reached the stage in the argument in which it is possible to understand why some such concept as that of 'the unconscious' had to be introduced and what function it would have to serve.

Freud is concerned to explain psychoneurotic symptoms as deriving from traumatic childhood experiences. He does not merely want to assert a causal connection between them, the evidence for which is an observable correlation of the one type of occurrence with the other. He wants to move to the level of a more general type of explanation in which both abnormal, psychoneurotic behaviour and normal behaviour are related to a multiplicity of antecedent conditions *via* a few simple theoretical concepts. 'The unconscious' is to fill the central role among these concepts. But, as we have already seen, the phenomena of human behaviour which this concept is to play its part in explaining fall *prima facie* within the province of neurophysiological explanation. And since Freud has been trained as a neurologist it is not surprising that he should have essayed to give such an explanation. The importance of this attempt by Freud is not simply historical. For I shall want to argue that neurophysiological explanation provided a model which had a formative influence on Freud's shaping of the concept of unconscious mental activity.

In 1895 Freud attempted to write a systematic account of psychology for neurologists. In it he constructed an explanatory system in which all mental phenomena are understood as resulting from the operation of certain material elements according to certain basic laws. It is a delightful and ingenious *tour de force* in which the contemporary discoveries of neurophysiology are skilfully blended with the preconceptions of that nineteenth-century materialism which took the schematism of Newtonian mechanics as the archetype of all authentically scientific explanation. On the one hand, Freud introduces the concept of the nerve-cell or neurone (the name given by Waldeyer in 1891) and its interconnection with other neurones. On the other hand, he understands these in typically reductionist fashion; the whole of mental life is to be understood in terms of the material and the mechanical. The formula 'matter in motion' is never very far in the background. (The prestige of this formula is perhaps best to be appreciated by reading Engel's *Anti-Dühring*.) Freud indeed defines a scientific psychology as one which conceives mental phenomena in terms of material states of affairs whose changes are susceptible of measurement and subject to laws of motion. The mind is to take its place among the inhabitants of the 'billiard-ball universe' of Newtonian mechanics.

The neurones are bearers of a quantitatively measurable excitation which is derived either from external stimuli or from within the body. Of this excitation to which Freud gives the non-committal descriptive label of Quantity two main things can be said. First, individual neurones tend to expel Quantity, to discharge excitation along the nerve-fibres. Secondly, the total amount of Quantity, the 'sum of excitation', as Freud and Breuer expressed a similar concept in their joint work, tends to remain constant. In terms of these two basic tendencies Freud works out a detailed account of the neuronic system. But before we come to consider the importance of the details of Freud's neurology, it is worth noting two points about the main structure. The first is that here we have a simple hydraulic model: Water in a system such that it flows from point to point, and enters and leaves the system at certain points, but remains constant in quantity within the system. The second is that such a model finds its use in suggesting new directions in which to seek explanation or new phenomena to be discovered. A simple example is the not dissimilar hydraulic model which Lorenz uses in explaining animal behaviour. The utility of Lorenz's model is that it enables us to correlate certain at first sight very different kinds of behavioural response to stimuli. But in Lorenz's case we are dealing with a model which is clearly a model and nothing more. Lorenz, for example, uses this model in explaining why, after responses have been evoked for some time, strength of response diminishes (the reservoir is almost empty) and why when the response has not been evoked for a long period it may be evoked without a stimulus at all (the reservoir is over-full). And in so far as the model covers an increasing range of the facts it will be taken more and more seriously. But at no point will it make sense to complain that we have no evidence for the existence of the 'water' or the 'reservoir'. To do this would be to suppose that we had to do with a reality rather than a model, with a hypothesis as to what goes on inside the animal rather than a way

of representing the facts of its behaviour, with a
'because' rather than an 'as if'. With Freud's
theory of the neurones it is quite the opposite.
Here we have a hypothesis, a straightforward
attempt to say what goes on in the nervous system.
And hence it does make sense to ask what the evidence is for the existence of whatever it is that flows
and what its nature is. If Freud had pressed these
questions he would have moved in the direction that
Sherrington and later neurologists have taken. But
this is not the type of question that Freud pressed
at all. He assumes his general theory of neurones
and Quantity in order to explain the specific phenomena in which he is interested. The important idea
which derives from the general structure of his
neurology is the idea that the amount of excitation
in the system remains constant: for in the notion
that whenever there is a loss of excitation the bal-
ance is restored we have the germ of the notion of
the human being as a system seeking equilibrium.
In neurophysiology this notion has lately become
of the first importance, but the neurophysiologists
owe nothing to Freud here. That the impulses trans-
mitted synaptically from neurone to neurone are
electrical in character; that electronic machines can
be built in which electronic cells play a role not dissimilar to neurones; that such machines can be self-
regulating by means of the device of negative feed-
back; that the nervous system might be conceived of
on the analogy of such a machine: these have been
the stages of the neurophysiological argument.
Freud was to carry over a concept of the personality

as a system seeking equilibrium into his later work, but he was to use it in quite a different way. Wherein this difference lies becomes clearer if we turn to look at the details of his theory of neurones. Then we shall be able to see how even when he abandoned this theory he was powerfully influenced by it.

It is important to note that the details of this early theory of Freud rest only on general considerations: they are not supported by any detailed appeal to the evidence of physiological observation and experiment. Secondly not only is his neurology speculative: it is neurology written up in psychological terms. In setting forth the workings of the nervous system the neurologist states at least the necessary and sometimes perhaps the sufficient causal conditions which must be satisfied if our mental life and our behaviour are to occur in the way that they do. But *qua* neurologist he is not concerned to describe that life and behaviour and the vocabulary appropriate to such descriptions does not figure in his reports except in so far as he is offering causal explanations of mental phenomena. It may be that when someone says 'I wish . . .' certain concomitant events occur in the nervous system. Saying whether this is so and what they are is part of neurology: but a wish is not itself a neurological event. Sometimes Freud writes as though he is observing this distinction but at other times he treats a wish as though it were part of, the 'subjective aspect' of, as though indeed it *were* a neurological event. So that the whole life of the mind becomes as it were one aspect of neurological processes and the language appropriate to its description suddenly appears inside a neurological account This is important because we shall shortly observe the same confusion in the reverse direction, the description of mental life and behaviour in terms more appropriate to neurophysiology.

Freud distinguishes three classes of neurones: φ neurones which allow excitation impulses to pass on in the system—they are the agency of perception; ψ neurones are permanently affected by what has passed through—they are the agency of memory; and ω neurones which are necessary for the retained memories or the impressed perceptions to become conscious. All the operations of mental life and of behaviour are functions of the flow of Quantity through these neurones. I do not propose to follow out Freud's account in detail but only to notice one major distinction which he finds himself forced to draw. The basic instinctual stimuli, which set going what Freud calls wishes, result in a flow of excitation which sometimes flows freely and sometimes is inhibited by that organization of neurones which Freud denominates 'the ego'. This inhibition by the ego prevents strong instinctual stimuli producing end-products indistinguishable from the end-products of stimuli from the external world. They prevent, that is to say, hallucinations. Freud names the uninhibited, free flow of excitation the 'primary processes' of his system and the inhibited, re-directed flow the 'secondary processes'. The primary processes are those which simply flow in such a way as to procure discharge from the neurones and the consequent satisfaction to the personality which Freud already identifies with Pleasure. The secondary processes are those by means of which distinctions are drawn between those stimuli which are external and those which are internal and instinctual. They lead us to distinguish and to come to terms with a determinate, external reality. We have here already the Pleasure principle and the Reality principle in conflict. 'Primary processes' are clearly primary in that the secondary are explained partly in terms of them and not *vice versa*. They are basic to Freud's neurological explanation and they are conceived of as determinate physical processes, as the transactions of identifiable physical entities which can be accurately located.

Although Freud abandoned finally and decisively the attempt at neurophysiological explanation shortly after constructing this 'highly complicated and extraordinarily ingenious working model of the mind as a piece of neurological machinery' (James Strachey's phrase), it is my contention and the most important contention in this part of my argument that Freud preserved the view of the mind as a piece of machinery and merely wrote up in psychological terms what had been originally intended as neurological theory. To make good this contention, we must now turn to Freud's first extended theoretical statement in 'The Interpretation of Dreams'.

Freud here has turned completely away from the physiological. He could write (1898): 'I have no inclination at all to keep the domain of the psychological floating, as it were, in the air, without any organic foundation. But I have no knowledge, neither theoretically nor therapeutically, beyond that conviction, so I have to conduct myself as if I had only the psychological before me.' Yet he retains in the seventh chapter of 'The Interpretation of Dreams' a great part of the theoretical structure used in his neurological writing. The 'wish' as the fundamental motive force of human beings, psychical energy distributed in various parts of a system, the distinction between primary and secondary processes and a great many other items survive the transition from neurology to psychology. This helps to explain the ease with which Freud slips into topographical language when speaking about the mind. Freud's picture of the mind as a series of places where various entities move about is, to borrow and distort an expression of Hobbes', 'the ghost of the central nervous system sitting crowned upon the grave thereof'. What Freud in fact does is to bring a scheme of explanation derived from neurology to the phenomena which his psychological studies had forced on his attention.

What are these phenomena? The symptoms of patients suffering from hysteria and obsessional neuroses, mature character traits such as Freud had investigated in the course of his own self-analysis— and dreams. It is a pity that when Freud came to set out his developed theory for the first time it was presented as primarily explanatory of the dream-material. But his subsequent statements make the resemblance between the explanation of dreams and that of neurotic symptoms unambiguously clear.

c

We have seen already how such concepts as 'repression' and 'trauma' had been introduced in connection with the latter. Now we have to see how they are built into Freud's developed explanation of the workings of the mind. In giving an account of that explanation my aim will be to exhibit as clearly as possible the logical structure of Freud's theory. Although therefore the ground which I am attempting to cover will be for the most part defined by the content of the Seventh Chapter of 'The Interpretation of Dreams' I shall follow my own order of exposition. This will fall into three parts. First, I shall have something to say about the character of the phenomena which the theory is designed to explain. Secondly, there is the actual set of concepts introduced to explain the phenomena. Thirdly, there is the question of the nature of the justification of this explanation which Freud offers.

First, then, the phenomena: we can see here a series of ever more detailed questions to which Freud is presenting a set of answers. Why do people behave neurotically, dream and so on? Because of past events in their lives and fundamentally because of certain childhood events. Why should such events cause neurotic behaviour? Because they lead to repression. What sort of events characteristically bring about repression? Why do neurotic symptoms have the specific character that they have? And so the questions could go on. Thus the material which Freud is attempting to explain is not just the occurrence of neurotic symptoms or dreams, but the correlation of earlier (traumatic) experiences with such

symptoms. Moreover, as with all scientific explanations that go beyond mere correlation, Freud's is
not an explanation simply of the abnormal and the
exceptional but also of the normal. The scope in
principle of Freudian explanation is all human behaviour: had it been less than this Freud would have
been unable to draw the famous comparison between
the effect of his own work and that of Copernicus. It
is not surprising therefore that happenings as normal
as dreams, slips of the tongue and jokes should re-
ceive attention along with melancholia, obsessive
habits, and excessive anxiety.

Secondly, the explanation of the phenomena.
Here the theoretical structure will be clearer if
generalized. Suppose some mental occurrence or
piece of behaviour which might be an obsessional
ritual, a dream or series of dreams, a slip of the
tongue, or what you will. The causal factors sufficient to produce it may be divided into those which
predisposed the subject to this kind of behaviour
and those which actually excited the behaviour. The
abnormality of neurotic behaviour consists in a dis-
proportion or incoherence between the exciting
causes and the behaviour. A man, for example,
breaks down on achieving the job for which he has
worked so long. But this example conceals the scale
of the incoherence. A man who suffers suddenly from
claustrophobic or kleptomanic behaviour, will not
seem to be reacting to anything in his situation. Part
of Freud's explanation of his or any other behaviour
is that no matter how improbable it may seem, all
behaviour is response to a particular situation de-

signed to secure the maximum of gratification and the minimum of pain from the situation. Freud's thesis that 'dreams are wish-fulfilments' is only part of a more general thesis that all behaviour is in a profound sense wish-fulfilment. We are therefore obliged to raise two questions: (i) What is it that conditions our wishes so that we can on occasion seek gratification in such strange ways? (ii) What sort of situation elicits such *prima facie* unlikely conduct? The answer to the first of these questions is that our fundamental desires are a product of instinctual desires and a variety of inhibitions and redirections of these desires. These desires are inhibited firstly by the demands of reality, and secondly by the painful character of certain situations which lead to a repression of the desire in its original direction and its redirection. The formative period of life is early childhood when the demands of reality take the shape first of biological needs and then of parental pressures and concessions. What happens to the child, not to speak of the child's own image of what happens to him, furnishes the material for traumatic events. Thus certain types of reaction to the world around him prove so painful to the child that the memory of them together with the emotion which expressed the instinctual desire behind the reaction are suppressed from consciousness. If the instinctual wish is to be fulfilled it must be fulfilled in some other way. There are therefore present in the personality as a result of these traumas of infancy *both* a set of memories so painful that they cannot be brought into consciousness by any normal means *and* a disposition to react to a certain type of a situation in a certain way, namely a way that will minimize the pain involved. Our adult behaviour is therefore explained in terms of the transformation of certain instinctual desires (which are unconscious and which are not to be identified with any biologically observable process). Where that transformation has been carried out with a minimum of conflict normal behaviour results: where the transformation is imperfect abnormal behaviour is the end-product. In dreams we admit censored, condensed, distorted versions of our unconscious desires and memories to the limited consciousness of the dream-world.

It is clear that the neurological distinction between primary and secondary processes has here been transferred from the physical to the mental without any great change except that we are no longer in the realm of the observable. The primary processes are still the realm of the uninhibited flow. Of this realm Dr. Ernest Jones writes: 'There reigns in it a quite uninhibited flow towards the imaginary fulfilment of the wish that stirs it—the only thing that can. It is unchecked by any logical contradiction, any causal associations; it has no sense of either time or of external reality. Its goal is either to discharge the excitation through any exit, or, if that fails, to establish a perceptual—if necessary, an hallucinatory—identity with the remembered perception of a previous satisfaction.' (*Sigmund Freud: Life and Work*, p. 436.)

The secondary processes are those in which the

checks of reality and pain have operated to redirect
the flow of psychical energy. In them too there is
still a seeking for an outlet in overt behaviour and
conscious awareness. But that outlet can only be
attained in ways compatible with the checks of
reality and pain. The process of thought is itself an
outcome of the secondary processes, a seeking after
the maximum satisfaction possible. 'All thinking,'
writes Dr. Jones, 'is no more than a complicated
and circuitous path towards the goal of wish-fulfilment.' 'Towards the goal of wish-fulfilment' because of the primary processes; 'complicated and
circuitous' because of the secondary.

The primary processes are not only primary in
that they are more fundamental to explanation;
they represent also the stage of early childhood, the
infantile stage of development, on which the secondary processes later impose themselves. Neurotic behaviour is a regression to the most basic modes of
reaction and thus also to infantile modes of reaction.
But before memories can be understood we must
return to the topic of repression.

How does the concept of repression function
within Freud's developed theory? Repression occurs
with the turning away from pain in the secondary
processes. (It is, I hope, unnecessary to point out
that the word 'pain' in the narrative is used to de-
note not physical pain, but the opposite of 'pleasure'. Dr. Jones, for instance, speaks of Unpleasure
where I have spoken of pain. But the contrast
'*Lust*' and '*Unlust*' seems to me the German equivalent to the English 'pleasure' and 'pain'.) What are

repressed are painful memories. 'Painful' here has a sexual connotation. That the flow of psychical energy is sexual in character and that mature sexuality emerges in the redirection of this flow by means of repression is evidenced for Freud in the attention paid to sexual matters in his patients' accounts of their traumatic experiences, in the discoveries made in the course of his self-analysis and in the analogy between the reactions of infancy and the sexual behaviour of adult life. Time and again in the analysis of actual dream-material in 'The Interpretation of Dreams' Freud is forced to bring out this analogy. But on this matter of sexuality Freud's ideas were still to develop in detail.

We have now reached the point at which it is possible to understand Freud's developed concept of the unconscious. About the unconscious we can make six points which decisively define its place and function.

(i) The Unconscious is formally distinguished from the Conscious and the Preconscious. The Preconscious is what, not being in consciousness, can be brought to consciousness by ordinary introspective methods. The Unconscious is the realm of that which cannot thus be brought into consciousness. Simply defined thus, 'the Unconscious' is defined in merely negative terms, and our understanding of what is to be meant by that term seems to depend on a prior understanding of what is meant by 'consciousness'. But in fact 'the Unconscious' is primarily defined in terms of the rest of Freud's theory so that difficult questions about the meaning of 'consciousness' need not necessarily be answered in order to understand what Freud means. Freud's own analogies and metaphors are sometimes positively unhelpful. When he says that 'the unconscious is the true psychical reality; in its inner nature it is just as unknown to us as is the reality of the outer world, and it is just as imperfectly communicated to us by the data of consciousness as is the outer world through the information reaching us from our sense organs' he seems to make the unconscious a kind of Kantian *ding-an-sich* which is inaccessible by definition. But to say things like this is to seem to make the Unconscious a merely negative category, an unknowable and therefore an incredible entity. In fact, Freud's concept is defined in positive terms by the reasons which lead him to adopt it. These reasons amount to nothing less than his total theoretical account. In so far as that account has justification the concept of the unconscious has justification. The only point that needs to be stressed about this definition is that the crucial line is that drawn between the Unconscious on the one hand and the Preconscious and the Conscious on the other.

(ii) The Unconscious is the area of the primary process. Some secondary processes are unconscious, but it is worth remembering that they are redirections of the primary process. Dr. Jones calls the primary process 'the kernel of the unconscious proper'. Without the concept of the primary process there would be no concept of the unconscious.

(iii) Freud himself said that the instructive contrast for an understanding of the unconscious is that between the *ego* and the *repressed*. Later Freud was to allow—what indeed seems implicit in what he says from the beginning—that there is that which is unconscious but was never repressed. But it remains true both that all that is repressed is unconscious and that an unconscious wish—Freud's basic and original conception of unconscious mental activity—is fundamentally a repressed wish. It is by understanding certain types of behaviour as the products of repression that Freud comes to understand them as products of the unconscious.

(iv) The Unconscious is the background link between infancy and adult life. Infantile sexuality, the patterning of psychical energy (libido) by infantile sexuality and repression, the subsequent form of unconscious wishes and the effect of all these both on the incidents of adult life and the permanent character traits of the adult—all are only comprehensible in Freud's terms by means of the concept of the Unconscious. It is because of what is unconscious that there is a *direct* causal effect of the infantile on the adult.

(v) The Unconscious is an omnipresent background to conscious and overt mental life and to behaviour. It exerts a continual causal influence upon conscious thought and behaviour. The form of Freud's concept of the Unconscious here derives partly from Freud's assumption of total determinism. Freud was to assert later that whenever a choice seems underived from sufficient, determining causes, this is only because we are unconscious of the factors determining our choice. The Unconscious is the place in which behaviour is determined.

(vi) The Unconscious is 'a place', 'a realm' (my terms). That is, in asserting the role of the Unconscious Freud is making an existential claim. He is not merely offering us an instructive diagram, a model in terms of which to envisage conscious thought and behaviour. He is propounding a hypothesis, asserting that the world includes an entity hitherto undiscovered. Freud himself and many of his expositors, talk of 'spatial metaphors', and clearly in ordinary language we often speak of the mind in spatial terms when we intend nothing spatial. We talk, for example, of thoughts 'passing through' or 'coming into' the mind. But in these cases we could easily replace our metaphors by non-spatial language. 'For a moment I thought . . .' or 'Suddenly I thought . . '. But Freud in explaining what he means is inexorably wedded to talk about processes, about happenings, about entities. So that even if we allow his spatial language to be metaphorical, we must not therefore see him as doing less than offering a hypothesis about some sort of existent reality.

In 1915 Freud produced a definitive metapsychological essay on 'The Unconscious'. To this we must give attention, if only for confirmation that the elucidation of the concept so far is correct. When Freud wrote this essay his theoretical conceptions had advanced in so far as a greater degree of system and amount of detail had been introduced. He was clearer about the place of the instincts, the mechanism of repression and so on. But the general structure that he had elaborated at the turn of the century remained, as it was to remain to the end. Freud's own explanation of his concept of the Unconscious is as follows.

'The Unconscious' is the name of a system of mental acts. The justification for belief in the existence of this system is two-fold: first, we are able to account for behaviour which cannot be accounted for in terms of conscious intentions; secondly, if we assume in psychoanalytic practise the existence of the Unconscious we are able to bring into consciousness contents of which the patient was unaware and in so doing we help to bring about the healing of his mental disorder. The distinction between the Unconscious properly so called and the Preconscious is then endorsed. What is in the Unconscious? First, in a loose sense, instincts are unconscious. In a loose sense, because instinctual impulses could never become conscious except in the form of something not themselves, that is in the form of ideas and emotions and because even in the Unconscious it is in the form of ideas (as the bearers of impulses) that the instincts take effect. Secondly, emotions are unconscious in a more specific sense. The suppression of feeling, of affect, from consciousness results in an unconscious disposition to give expression to such feeling, although the form of that expression will vary from case to case. As a result of repression an emotional impulse may be transferred from one idea to another, or it may simply be dammed up, awaiting a possible release when a suitable idea presents itself. In this respect unconscious emotions differ sharply from ideas. An idea that is unconscious survives 'as an actual formation in the system Ucs'. To bring an idea into consciousness it is not enough for someone simply to become aware of the idea. An analyst, for example, may tell a patient something that the patient has forgotten because he has repressed an idea. But although the patient has been introduced to an idea which is in his unconscious he has not thereby made the idea conscious. To do that he must bring out into consciousness his own unconscious idea. ('You still fear your father' the analyst may say. But the patient's reception of this, his agreeing to it even, is different from his becoming aware of his own idea of his father as an object of hate.) 'Ideas' therefore are not to be identified with propositions. They are discrete mental entities which although they may be verbalized correctly in a certain form of words are still sharply distinguishable from other ideas which are similarly verbalizable.

Ideas and emotions are repressed. Why? Freud's own example is taken from anxiety-hysteria. A child tries to express a love-impulse which springs from the Unconscious. The reception of this attempt is so painful (the parent rejects the love offered) that the impulse is repressed. What happens in repression is that the idea ('love-of-the-parent') is rejected into the Unconscious and the emotion is displayed as an objectless anxiety. But this is unmanagable by the Preconscious and so the emotion attaches itself to a substitutive idea 'which on the one hand was connected by association with the rejected idea, and, on the other, escaped repression by reason of its remoteness from that idea (displacement substitute), and which permitted of a rationalization of the still uncontrollable outbreak of anxiety'. This substitution idea could be, for example, the kind of thing that occurs in an animal phobia. Here the idea of the feared animal both, by being a substitute for it, assists in the repression of the idea originally attached to the love-impulse and allows an outlet for the anxiety. Love of the parent has been transformed into fear of the animal. The repressed idea retains in the Unconscious its original character. The repressed emotion becomes dischargable in another form. I have here expanded Freud's example a little without, I hope, distorting it, because it brings out clearly what is most relevant to my theme in this essay, namely the distinctions between the different kinds of content which occur in the Unconscious. In the next to penultimate section of his essay, Freud restates the omnipresent causal influence of the Unconscious on both the Preconscious and the Conscious, while emphasizing those characteristics of the Unconscious which relate it to his earlier description of primary processes: '*exemption from mutual contradiction*, *primary process* (motility of cathexis), *timelessness*, and *substitution* of *psychic for external reality*—these are the characteristics which we may expect to find in processes belonging to the system Ucs'. Freud goes on to say that 'Unconscious processes can only be observed by us under the conditions of dreaming and of neurosis . . .' and all these characteristics can be well understood in terms of dreams. For in dreams we conjoin what are in fact mutually incompatible states of affairs, strong emotions become attached to all sorts of objects and are easily transferred, the ordinary time sequence is sometimes disordered or reversed and we replace the objects of the external world with an environment of mental constructs. But Freud reserves another characteristic of the Unconscious for mention in the context of schizophrenic derangement of language. In schizophrenia phrases and sentences are used outside any context that would make them ordinarily intelligible. What has happened according to Freud is that the idea normally attached by the user to the expression in question has been of such a kind that it has been repressed into the Unconscious. The verbal expression of the idea becomes detached from what Freud calls the concrete idea. Freud concludes from this that an essential difference between a conscious and an unconscious idea is that the former is necessarily expressed in words but the latter is not. It is something preverbal, potentially verbalizable, but not itself a matter of words: 'the conscious idea comprises the concrete idea plus the verbal idea corresponding to it, whilst the idea is that of the thing alone'. There is a certain obscurity in this statement, but Freud is at least saying that the unconscious is a realm of entities ('ideas') which if they become conscious do so by means of verbal expression. His use of 'idea', as we have noted earlier, is reminiscent of the philosophical vocabulary of Brentano, or for that matter of Locke.

We can summarize the whole matter by saying that in dreams and psychoneurotic behaviour we find modes of expression and types of action which can only be explained on the supposition that as well as our conscious mental activity and what is not but can be readily made available in the form of conscious mental activity, there is a realm of unconscious mental activity where ideas charged with psychical energy combine and substitute for one another in a variety of ways. Ideas of a psychically painful kind are repressed into the unconscious, notably in the period of early childhood development. Such ideas have a predominantly sexual character. Adult character traits, normal as well as neurotic, are determined by past success and failure in coping with childhood development and present success and failure in achieving a compromise between the demands of external social reality and the unconscious. The nature of this compromise will be expressed in one's dreams and personal habits, and failure to achieve success here will result in neurosis or psychosis depending on the degree of failure. On the basis of observation of the symptoms of neurotic and psychotic breakdown Freud constructs his theory which he gradually extends to cover all normal behaviour, disclosing a variety of implications from his general theory for the explanation of the genesis of artistic activity, religious belief and so on. But it is not my concern to pursue these fascinating corollaries of Freud's general theory.

What I hope I have so far succeeded in doing is to exhibit the place which one central concept holds in that theory, the concept of unconscious mental activity. For to have understood precisely what Freud had in his own mind when he spoke of 'The Unconscious' is a necessary preliminary to examining the nature and status of Freud's concept.

CHAPTER THREE

MENTAL WORDS AND MENTAL CONCEPTS

IN order to make it clear what legitimate doubts may be raised about Freud's presentation of the concept of the unconscious, it is important to understand why a type of objection that has often been alleged against that concept cannot in fact be sustained. This type of objection can be stated as follows. Terms such as 'wish', 'motive', 'fear', 'desire', it is said, refer to features of ordinary conscious mental life and all our ordinary use of these terms presupposes that this is so. When we talk of someone as having dishonourable motives or haunting fears we mean—in part, at least—that they experience in their minds certain thoughts, and it is because we mean this that we condemn or sympathize with them. When we assess someone's actions in moral terms, we often inquire as to his intentions, what he wished to do, what his motives were: the implication of this is that the moral agent's intentions and the like were such that he was fully aware of them at the time and is in a position to declare what they were. But if this is so no

sense can be attached to these terms if they are pre-
fixed by the adjective 'unconscious'. These terms,
that is, essentially refer to or describe conscious
states and to suggest that those states could be unconscious is to attempt to speak of 'unconscious
conscious states'.

This objection has often been pressed in even more
general terms. It has been argued not only that
wishes, motives and the like cannot be unconscious,
but that nothing can be. For that of which we are
unconscious is that of which *ex hypothesi* we are and
must be unaware. But of that of which we cannot be
aware nothing can be known or said: it cannot therefore be known or said to exist. The philosophers who
advanced this type of argument against Freud only
displayed their own naïvete in assuming that linguistic objections of so obvious a kind could have
been ignored by Freud. But they make it plain that
what is crucial is to exhibit the sense that
the term 'unconscious' has in psychoanalytic theory
and to exhibit what sort of evidence it is on the
basis of which the occurrence of unconscious mental
activity is asserted. Yet to accept the demand that
this should be done is not necessarily to accept the
assumptions of those who raise this type of objection. Indeed a first step should be precisely to
examine their assumptions as to how ordinary
mental words are used. Freud is accused of innovating in his use of 'unconscious'. But on what is
he innovating?

The most obviously important fact for our purposes is that among the ordinary terms used to des-

cribe mental activity 'unconscious' and its cognate terms already figure.

The pre-Freudian meanings of 'unconscious' fall under two main headings: (i) 'Unconscious' as an adjective applied to things as distinct from people (equivalent to 'inanimate') and to those in a state of trance or coma as distinct from those in a normal waking condition. This latter is perhaps the primary sense of 'unconscious', which leads on to the more interesting class of meanings from our point of view, namely (ii) 'unconscious of' or more commonly 'unconsciously' where there is an essentially adverbial qualification of some expression referring to an activity or piece of behaviour. Here there are a set of different shades of meaning that have to be distinguished. Sometimes 'unconsciously' means 'without conscious intention'. W. B. Yeats quotes his father as saying 'I must paint what I see in front of me. Of course I shall really paint something different because my nature will come in unconsciously.' And this use carries a flavour not just of 'without conscious intention' but also of 'without conscious effort'. But it does not suggest that J. B. Yeats was not aware of what was appearing on the canvas in front of him. This however is sometimes suggested by 'unconsciously', not that we are merely unaware of any conscious intention to do what we do, but that we are unconscious of what we are doing. Thus T. L. Peacock in 'Gryll Grange' makes Dr. Opimian describe how Lord Curryfin transferred his devotion from Miss Gryll to Miss Niphet before he realized what he had done by saying: 'The young lord went on some time, adhering as he supposed, to his first pursuit, and falling unconsciously and inextricably into the second. . . .' These examples help to bring out two interesting features of ordinary usage. The first is that 'unconscious' and its cognates are often ambiguous: sometimes to call an activity unconscious is to say that it is unknown, sometimes that it is performed unknowingly. This ambiguity which was to be perpetuated by Freud is sometimes concealed by the fact that in calling some piece of mental activity unconscious it is suggested *both* that it is carried on without conscious intention, that it is unknowing, *and* that it is such that it is unknown, at least to the agent, and perhaps to others as well. But these two claims must be distinguished. What is involved in this distinction will be seen presently. Secondly, when 'unconsciously' is used as equivalent to 'inadvertently' it figures among those adverbs which may be invoked to excuse otherwise blameworthy behaviour. Thus ordinary language, in this case at least uninfected by metaphysics or psychology, lends itself easily to the suggestions, that a man's behaviour may be, to use the psychologist's jargon, goal-directed, but that he may not perceive the goal to which his behaviour is tending: he is thus said both to have unconscious (undirected, unintended) purposes and to be unconscious of (unaware of, ignorant of) his purposes. He himself, or others may become conscious of what he is up to and then he will have the choice of making his purpose a conscious one (and 'conscious of' and 'conscious' correspond respectively to the latter and the former uses of 'unconscious' in the previous sentence) or of abandoning it. Until he becomes conscious of his purpose, he cannot be blamed for pursuing it, for indeed except in a somewhat metaphorical sense he is not pursuing it. How far does Freud follow ordinary language here?

Sometimes, very closely. One outstanding point about the pre-Freudian use of 'unconscious' is its high incidence in the writings of the more sensitive novelists. Henry James abounds in phrases like 'a nature all unconsciously grateful' (*Roderick Hudson*), or 'the unconscious violence offered by her nature to his every memory of her mother' (*The Awkward Age*), and the idea recurs even more often than the word. Nor is this merely accidental. One of the central features of the novel is the depicting of how much of human action and passion is not the fruit of conscious intention. This uncovering of our own ignorance of ourselves Freud did not fail to see that he shared with the imaginative writer. As early as 1895 he wrote: 'I have not always been a psychotherapist . . and it still strikes me as strange that the case histories I write should read like *short stories* and that, as one might say, they lack the serious stamp of science. I must console myself with the reflection that the nature of the subject is evidently responsible for this rather than any preference of my own. The fact is that local diagnosis and electrical reactions lead nowhere in the study of hysteria, whereas the detailed description of mental processes *such as we are accustomed to find in the works of imaginative writers* enables me, with the use of a few psychological formulas, to obtain at least some kind of insight into the course of that affection.' This recognition by Freud of his place as being among the imaginative describers of human behaviour is striking; and it will be one of the main theses of this essay that in essays such as this Freud gave a correct account of his discoveries and of his method of achieving them. But clearly there are many other places where Freud speaks with a different voice. In a passage already quoted Freud describes his work as discovering 'the scientific method by which the unconscious can be studied'. And here he uses 'unconscious' in a way that it is never used in ordinary language, as a noun, and not as adjective or adverb. Here there is radical innovation. For where Freud uses 'unconscious' and 'unconsciously' he extends (although how far he extends we have yet to note) earlier uses of these words; but when he speaks of '*the* unconscious' he invents a new term for which he has to prescribe a meaning and a use. And in this innovation he is curiously dominated by a picture of the mind which he at many points explicitly rejected.

To claim that Freud's theory of unconscious mental activity must be at fault because wishes, motives, fears and the like must be conscious is, I have argued, mistaken. The terms 'wish', 'fear' and so on do not in ordinary usage describe and refer to only private moments of consciousness, to inner mental events, but are in part at least—and it is an essential part—descriptive of patterns of behaviour which are publicly observable. These patterns may go unrecognized and so be denominated 'unconscious'. But if it is allowed that this is how such words ordinarily function, then we come into sharp conflict with that philosophical picture of mind which derives largely from Descartes and which has been dubbed by Professor Gilbert Ryle 'the ghost in the machine'. Maritain spoke instead of 'the angel in the machine' and this is in some ways more apt. For the mind on this view is not merely separate and distinct from the body, but it knows itself directly in a way that it knows nothing else, and it knows itself through and through. Its own acts are manifest to it with a pellucid and intuitive self-evidence. Not only this but the mind is above all the seat of intellect, of the self-consciously rational in man. Now Freud clearly does not think of man as possessing this kind of rational self-knowledge in his ordinary consciousness, and in so far as he does not do this he rejects the Cartesian picture of the mind. But Freud retains from the Cartesian picture the idea of the mind as something distinct and apart, a place or a realm which can be inhabited by such entities as ideas. Only he makes dominant not 'the conscious' mind but 'the unconscious'. He introduces 'unconscious' as an adjective to describe what we may have hitherto observed but have not hitherto recognized or classified. He introduces 'the unconscious' as a noun not to describe, but to explain.

This then is the second source we have found for Freud's substantial picture of the unconscious mind.

The Cartesian philosophical tradition, mediated by Brentano, reinforces and is reinforced by his depicting of the unconscious in terms which he had elaborated to deal with the entities of neurophysiology. The conception of unconscious ideas as non-physical entities is an odd one, largely because the conception of ideas as entities is odd. And if Freud's statements about the unconscious and its contents are understood as hypotheses about such inaccessible entities, the objection that being unconscious such contents must be inaccessible to knowledge might have some point. But it is not necessary to understand them thus. Certainly the unconscious and its contents are *ex hypothesi* unobservable, and if philosophy were still at the stage when positivism was waging a war to the death against unobservables no doubt the whole conception of the unconscious would have to be rejected. But the positivism that rejected unobservables in so wholesale a fashion was not merely too *a priori* in its framing of criteria by which concepts were to be judged legitimate or the reverse; it was also profoundly in error as to the character of scientific theorizing. For in such theorizing concepts which refer to unobservables have a legitimate, important and necessary place. And in elucidating the nature of the concept of the unconscious the possibility that it is a concept of this kind must be taken very seriously.

In framing scientific explanations, we are not merely concerned to state the occurrence of certain regularities in nature. The discovery that certain types of event are regularly found conjoined is rather a preliminary to explanation. We explain such regularities by putting forward hypotheses from which the occurrence of the regularities in question can be deduced. Thus the regularities in the behaviour of gases under specified conditions which are asserted in Boyle's Law and Dalton's Law of Partial Pressures can be explained on the hypothesis that gases are composed of small particles of particular kinds interacting according to the laws of Newtonian mechanics. The basic requirement for a scientific theory is not that it shall refer to nothing but observables but that statements which are about observables and therefore verifiable by observation or experiment shall be deducible from it. But this is not enough. The theory must not merely be such that the statements concerning the regularities which it was originally introduced to explain are deducible from it. We must also be able if the explanation of the regularities with which we were originally concerned is correct, to deduce further statements of a testable kind, the verifying of which constitutes the confirmation of the hypothesis. The more that can be deduced from a particular hypothesis the better the scientist will be pleased; for the search for more and more general types of explanation is of the essence of scientific theorizing. A scientific theory therefore may have a number of layers. The statements of which it is made up can be arranged on a deductive pattern with the more general and logically complex at the top, the observation-statements at the bottom. Concepts which refer to unobservables will have a place on the higher steps of the deductive ladder if by using them we can formulate assertions from which observation statements can be deduced which are true and which could not be deduced from the theory unless such assertions were included. Commonplace examples of such concepts are those of the electron and of the gene. The concept of the unconscious perhaps possesses a similar logical status.

At this point however it has to be remembered that there have also been concepts of this kind which have been discredited because no observable consequences, or at least no further observable consequences than those which they had originally been introduced to explain, could be deduced from the asertions in which they found a place. Such was the concept of the ether. Whether the unconscious is to be classed with the electron as a notion of great explanatory power or with the ether as a bogus and empty theoretical concept is therefore the crucial question.

We can now see that this inquiry about Freud's conception of unconscious mental activity necessarily falls into two parts. First, there are Freud's additions to the catalogue of mental events, whereby unconscious wishes, anxieties and the like appear as well as conscious ones. Here Freud extends ordinary language, but ordinary language provides a foundation for his work. And his work is at this point a work of description. So that the question to be raised about his concepts is whether he succeeds in using them to describe what without them could only be described inadequately or perhaps not at all.

Secondly, Freud does not merely add to the list of mental states and events. He provides an explanation of those events and of their relation to the events of early childhood. In this explanation the term 'the unconscious', which expresses a conceptual innovation by means of a linguistic one, has a key theoretical role. So that we have not only to deal with 'unconscious' as a descriptive term, but with 'the unconscious' as an explanatory concept. These two distinct inquiries must be raised about Freud's account of unconscious mental activity.

CHAPTER FOUR

DESCRIBING AND EXPLAINING

FREUD'S theories fall half-way between two brilliant but wrongheaded monolithic attempts to account for human behaviour, which have shared between them the task of correcting the Cartesian theory of mind. On the one hand there is the view that Descartes was right in seeing the physical world as a world of mechanical causation, wrong in seeing the mental world as exempt from its impact except through the slender medium of the pineal gland. What has to be done is to assimilate the explanation of mental states and occurrences to the explanation of physical states and occurrences. The eighteenth-century exponents of this view such as Diderot and de Lamettrie find their contemporary heirs in the American 'behaviour-theorists' such as Tolman and Hull whose various theories of learning seek to exhibit behaviour as consisting in a set of responses to external stimuli, the nature and quality of the response being determined by predisposing causal factors. These theories have so far only found a whole precise exemplification in the behaviour of rats, but their application to human beings has generally been considered by their exponents as only a matter of time, effort and experiment. At the other extreme, there are those who admire the Cartesian autonomy of mind so much that they regret any suggestion of dependence upon or interrelation with the physical at all. Such are the French existentialists of the present day, Sartre and his disciples. For Sartre all important human behaviour is the fruit of human decision. You are what you are because of what you have decided. This is asserted not just of actions but also of attitudes and emotions. Your sadness is the result of your choosing to be sad. There are no antecedent conditions which determine human behaviour. The difficulty with both of these positions is that each conflicts with some quite undeniable feature of human behaviour. For clearly on the one hand the work of appraisal and argument that goes on in the mind affecting and altering all our conduct can never be adequately described in terms of stimulus and response if only because—a Kantian insight—the validity of reasons as reasons cannot be dealt with in causal terms. On the other hand a great deal of the life of the mind clearly takes the shape that it does because of formative environmental and biological conditions. But equally clearly each of these positions states a legitimate starting-point for approaching human behaviour. One may ask 'Why?' and expect an answer in terms of reasons, intentions, purposes and the like; or one may ask 'Why?' and expect an answer in terms of physiological or psychological determining antecedent conditions. This

dichotomy remains untouched when the misleading character of other dichotomies such as that
between the mental and the physical, or the inner
and the outer aspects of human behaviour, has been
noted.

Freud approached this dichotomy in paradoxical
fashion, seeing intentions and purposes where the
pre-Freudian would have seen only causes, and
seeing causes where the pre-Freudian would have
seen none. His treatment of the intentional aspects
of human behaviour is notable. The issue about
intention and related concepts is apt to be treated
by contemporary philosophers as a Ryle versus
Descartes issue. And they usually want to conclude
that here both Ryle and Descartes are in some sense
right. Professor J. A. Passmore, for example, speaks
of two different models. On the view suggested by
one model—'let us call it the "coherence model"—
a course of action is "intended" whenever it shows
a pattern, working towards a satisfying culminating
point which can be picked out as "its purpose"
or "the intention behind the actions". A second
model, however—let us call it the "planning"
model—assimilates intending to deliberately planning a course of action.' Freud uses both these
models, assigning to them different and comple-
mentary functions rather than seeing them as
alternatives between which he must shift uneasily,
as so many contemporary philosophers seem to see
them.

The difficulty is this. Clearly a man may intend
to go through a series of actions which have become

habitual to him. So he may perform them without thinking about them, as a man may eat his dinner while thinking about stock market prices. But a man who eats his dinner thus, does not eat it unintentionally, as he might, through similar absent-mindedness, drink his neighbour's coffee unintentionally. He intended to eat his dinner, but he never formulated this intention in his mind. So a man may intend to do something and do it, without any inner mental planning constituting 'his intention'. This suggests that when we say 'he intended to . . .' we mean that we recognize a pattern of purpose in his actions, whatever he said to himself about them. Equally we often ask what the author or the artist intended when confronted with a puzzling piece of work. And exegetes and critics attempt to answer this question not by speculating about what went on in the author's or artist's mind, but by studying the work more closely and attempting to find some coherent pattern in it. This sort of case provides Passmore with an additional argument for adopting his first or 'coherence' model.

There are at least two sorts of case however which can be cited against this model. When we say that someone is attempting to deceive us as to his intentions, we mean that he says one thing to himself but another to us, and that he seeks not to betray in his actions anything of the purpose which he holds in his mind. And here we clearly contrast the 'intention' which is a piece of mental planning, of thinking with the outward actions whatever they are. Again, very often our intentions are frustrated: what we have planned is never put into operation. Here there are no actions to correspond to the preliminary mental planning. So the 'intention' is what went on in the mind. This type of consideration suggests the second of Passmore's models.

Before looking at the importance of this dilemma for Freud, three further points must be made about it. The first is that it will not do simply to suggest that the one model is appropriate for some types of situations, the other for others. The reason why this is inadequate is that, although sometimes we discover a man's intentions by asking him what they are and sometimes by observing his behaviour and sometimes by both, we do not mean something different by 'intention' in each of these cases. It may be that slightly different situations are grouped together by use of the same form of words 'he intended to . . . ' but there is at least, and perhaps more than a family resemblance between them. Secondly, 'I intend to . . .' is not simply the first person of the third person 'he intended to . . . '. When I say 'he intended to . . .' I describe something, perhaps his actions, perhaps his mental projects, perhaps both; but when I say 'I intend to . . .' I do not describe anything at all. My intending is not something described or referred to by saying 'I intend to . . .'; it simply *in one sense* is my saying 'I intend to . . .', whether I say this aloud or only think it. But there are clearly cases where my intentions, as constituted by what I say or think, are at variance with the intentions which are apparent in my actions. A man involved in an unhappy love affair who tells his friends that he intends to break free from it, but who continues to see the girl and to send her gifts—what are we to say his intentions in fact are? We might say a number of things: that he was insincere in what he said, that he was ignorant of his own intentions, that he had two conflicting intentions. But there are criteria to be applied in deciding what to say here. What we ought to say surely is that the man has two conflicting intentions, unless either there is positive evidence that he is insincere or (the more interesting case from our point of view) he appears unable to recognize a conflict between what he says and what he does. Here we may say that he is ignorant of his intentions, but perhaps it is clear to say that he has one intention consciously, but another of which he is unaware or unconscious. Before we allow this use of 'unconscious' to lead us back to Freud, a third point must be noted. This dilemma is not merely about the word 'intention' and its application; it extends to all those words which have to do with the intentional and purposive aspects of human behaviour. 'Purpose', 'motive', 'wish', 'desire' all have this double interpretation. It was indeed in terms of 'motive' that the contemporary discussion was mainly conducted by Ryle and his critics. For Ryle, a motive is a disposition to behave in a certain way under certain conditions. To ascribe a motive, therefore, is to say something about behaviour, about tendencies to behave in a particular manner. Mr. D. J. McCracken, among others, has argued that motives are, at least on occasion, occurrences rather than

E

(or as well as) dispositions. Macbeth's ambition was what went on in Macbeth's mind which led him to act as he did. Here in the case of 'motive' all the moves that we have made in the case of 'intention' could be made over again. To say that 'motive', 'intention', 'wish' and so on resemble each other in this way is not of course to ignore their differences. But for our purposes for the moment the resemblances are more important. How, then, does all this relate to Freud's treatment of the intentional aspects of human behaviour?

Freud argues that certain types of neurotic behaviour are the result of unconscious motivation. The neurotic has purposes and intentions of which he is unaware. Since he is unaware of them, he cannot avow them. Freud would seem to be using 'intention' here to refer to a pattern of behaviour. But an essential feature of psychoanalysis is the way in which the neurotic comes to recognize and to acknowledge the purpose of his acts. It is only when this has come about that he is able to redirect his intentions, to alter his behaviour in the light of his new self-knowledge. This acknowledgement by the patient confirms the analyst's interpretation of the motivation of the neurotic behaviour. And unless the patient will *in the end* avow his intention the analyst's interpretation of his behaviour is held to be mistaken. 'In the end' is a phrase that covers the multitude of almost interminable turnings and twistings of which an analysis may consist. Of course, it is a feature of the psychoneuroses that the patient will in the short run deny, and often deny vehemently, the analyst's interpretations of his conduct. Sometimes this denial may go on for a very long time. And there are unsuccessful analyses. So that it will not do for the psychoanalyst to make it a necessary criterion of a correct interpretation of the motivation of an action that the patient should in fact avow the correctness of the interpretation within any particular period of time. But the psychoanalyst *means* by a correct interpretation of an action an interpretation that the patient *would* avow if only certain conditions were to be fulfilled. What these conditions are depends on the character of the patient's disorder and its aetiology. Thus a patient's intention or purpose in his neurotic behaviour is something which both is betrayed in his behaviour and is what he would, if he were not prevented by his disorder, avow. Thus the meaning of 'intention' is elucidated by a categorical reference to behaviour supplemented by a hypothetical reference to avowals. This surely is how the concept of intention and kindred concepts ought to be understood in ordinary pre-Freudian usage.

When we ascribe an intention, purpose or motive to someone, we do more than assert a tendency to behave in a particular way or a pattern in their actions. What more we do is brought out by distinguishing between statements about causal properties and statements about the dispositions of human beings, where 'dispositions' still bears its ordinary meaning. The evidence required to justify the assertion that 'salt is soluble in water' is simply that it has so dissolved; whereas the evidence re-

quired to justify the assertion that 'Smith is ambitious' is always more than that he has behaved in
an ambitious fashion. The relevant difference between
salt and Smith, between things and people, is perhaps no more than that people can talk about their
behaviour. And in the end it would be relevant to
ask Smith about his behaviour. For it always makes
sense to say that Smith seems to be ambitious, because he behaves in certain ways, but that he may
not in fact be ambitious; it would be nonsense to
say of salt that it dissolved and would therefore
seem to be soluble but might not be. Asking Smith
himself is not the only thing that would be relevant.
We would watch his further behaviour and the extent to which he behaved consistently. But the crucial test would still be Smith's response when we
asked him about his ambition. If Smith avowed his
ambition we should have all the evidence that we
needed and indeed all the evidence that it was possible to have. If Smith denied his ambition, the
onus would be on him to provide us with a plausible
alternative explanation of his behaviour. If he could
do this, we should have to revise our verdict. If he
could not, we should have a case of unconscious
ambition in the ordinary pre-Freudian sense of 'unconscious'. If on pointing this out in suitable ways
to Smith, we discovered an inability in Smith to recognize his own ambition, we should have a case of
unconscious ambition in something more like the
Freudian sense of 'unconscious'. (For the purpose of
illustration it does not matter that 'unconscious'
for the Freudian would qualify not something like

'ambition' but something like 'fear of his father'.)
And if Smith's denial of his trait was especially vehement we should perhaps treat this as almost as
conclusive as an avowal. Incidentally, in ordinary
attributions of motive and intention we find exactly
the same tendency to treat avowals as confirming
but denials as not necessarily overthrowing our
interpretations that we find in the psychoanalyst's
treatment of the patient's response to his interpretations. Those who have criticized Freud and his
followers for acting thus have missed this link
between the treatment of unconscious motives in
ordinary speech and their treatment by Freud. This
link, as I have urged, is that both elements of
intentional action—the pattern in the behaviour
and the possibility of avowal, are essential in both
the ordinary and the Freudian applications of the
concepts of motive and intention. All those cases in
which philosophers have seen an intention which is
only a pattern of behaviour are cases where the agent
would avow the intention if certain conditions were
fulfilled. And thus the fact that his intention may
not actually occur as a piece of conscious mental
activity is irrelevant. What matters is what would
happen *if* the agent were to be pressed on the matter.
Freud's perceptive use of the concept thus throws
light on our ordinary language. The difference
between neurotic motives and purposes and non-
neurotic is a difference in the conditions which
would have to be fulfilled in order for the agent to
be able to avow his motives and purposes. But in the
end an intention is something that must be capable

of being avowed. To look at Freud therefore is to bring out the truth of a passage in Wittgenstein's *Philosophical Investigations* (247) which has incurred criticism from Passmore: '"Only you can know if you had that intention". One might tell someone this when one was explaining the meaning of the word "intention" to him. For then it means: *that* is how we use it. (And here "*know*" means that the expression of uncertainty is senseless).' The student of Freud will note that Wittgenstein said '*can* know' and not '*do* know'.

I have laboured this point about the common element in the pre-Freudian and in Freud's concepts because it will help to make clear what Freud is in fact doing when he ascribes to a piece of behaviour unconscious motivation. Now Freud is often conceptually confused, especially in his more theoretical writings. Professor A. G. N. Flew has drawn our attention to a passage (*Introductory Lectures*, p. 234) where Freud uses 'motive' in 'unconscious motive' in the way I have suggested and underlines the fact by using 'purpose' as a synonym for 'motive'. Mr. Peter Alexander has pointed out that in this very same passage Freud calls the unconscious motive 'the driving force behind the act'. In other words, he tries to treat unconscious motives both as purposes and as causes. This is simply a confusion. Contemporary psychologists normally use 'motive' and 'motivation' in ascribing causes: ordinary language in ascribing purposes. Freud's vocabulary falls betwixt and between. But in practice when Freud ascribes an unconscious motive to an action he ascribes a purpose. That purpose is unconscious if it is not only unacknowledged (that alone would merely make it preconscious) but if the patient is unable by ordinary means to acknowledge it. It is this inability of the patient which introduces a genuine causal element into the explanation of the behaviour in question. But if the prestige of causal explanations makes us rush past the ascriptions of purpose in order to concentrate attention on Freud's causal explanation of the neurotic patient's inability to recognize his symptoms for what they are, and to control and to alter his behaviour we shall miss a whole dimension in Freud's achievement. For an essential part of Freud's achievement lies not in his explanations of abnormal behaviour but in his redescription of such behaviour.

What did Freud do? Not just suggest a set of causes for the data, the neurotic symptoms and the rest, but tell us for the first time what the data were. The concept of 'wish-fulfilment' which we have seen to be so important in Freud's theoretical structure is not genuinely a causal concept. To describe something, a belief or a piece of behaviour, as an example of wish-fulfilment is to discern a purpose in belief or behaviour, a gratification secured by it or a painful situation avoided, not a driving force behind belief or behaviour. Or rather, it is only when we state antecedent conditions given which the agent could not but seek such gratification in some such way as this that we turn wish-fulfilment into a causal concept. So that Freud's ordinary concept of unconscious motive is both of cause behind and purpose in the neurotic condition, obsessional ritual or hysterical paralysis. The patient performs an obsessional ritual, say, before going to sleep. Jugs, clocks, anything that might fall or make a noise must be removed from the room. When all is done, then the room must once again be inspected to make sure that nothing has been left undone. When the light is put out, presently it must go on again, for a further inspection. Pre-Freudians, we say that this unaccountable behaviour is such that the patient is unable to sleep and so to have a normal life. Freud points out that the patient performs the ritual in order not to sleep. The ritual expresses the patient's fearful avoidance of sleep. Then he accounts for this attitude of the patient by a causal explanation in terms of what the patient experienced when as a child she woke in the dark and when she was taken into her parent's bed. His recognition of purpose is logically independent of his causal explanation. But when Freud refers to the patient's behaviour as unconsciously motivated he compresses the two parts of his explanation into one. Distinguishing the two carefully, and attempting to underline Freud's preoccupation with purposes and intentions, his stress on causes must nonetheless not be neglected. But before we turn to examine this element of causal explanation in Freud's thought, let us first look more closely at his work of description.

Professor A. G. N. Flew, among others, has pointed to the analogy between the way in which a great novelist is concerned with human behaviour and the way in which Freud was concerned with it. But a novelist would not have an intelligible narrative to present if he did not present at least a hard core of intelligible action, of consciously acknowledged purposes. Even those novelists most aware of how much of human reality is opaque, Marcel Proust and Henry James, portray the shadows of misunderstanding against a light of comprehension. But Freud systematically explores the puzzling, the hitherto unintelligible and the abnormal in human life to such a degree that he alters completely the boundary between the intelligible and the unintelligible. In the pre-Freudian, the novelist's, use of 'unconscious', what is unconscious is what the agent does not recognize, although others may. In Freud's use what is unconscious goes unrecognized for what it is both by the agent and by everyone else—until Freud fashions his own diagnostic technique. We have already quoted the passage in which he notes the resemblance of his methods to those of the imaginative writer. But, as with imaginative writing, Freud does not in this part of his work amass evidence for a conclusion. He tells us what he sees and what to look for. And if we cannot see too, he is also (here he differs from the novelist) able to note a purpose in our own blindness. In doing this Freud alters our notions of what hysteria or neurotic obsessions are. They are attempts to seek gratification or to avoid pain which go unrecognized both by the agent and by others.

In psychoanalytic therapy the patient has to

recognize his disorder as what it is, and then by identifying his behaviour correctly he is put in a better position for altering it. But recognition of the purposive character of his behaviour is not enough to alter it. The reason for this is as follows. Neurotic behaviour is, according to Freud, essentially regressive. That is, it is behaviour of a kind appropriate to certain key situations in early childhood, and this thesis must not be confused with the thesis with which Freud allies it, namely that the ultimate predisposing causes of regressive behaviour are failures to cope with just such key childhood situations, those for example involved in weaning, in potting training and in jealousy over parental love. Freud both described regressive behaviour as childlike and explained it as originating from childhood. But the situation is even more complex than this. For the patient comes to recognize the true nature of his neurotic behaviour, to see that it is regressive, by recalling by means of free association the original traumatic childhood situation which his adult actions are reproducing. It is important to remember here that it is no use the patient's simply coming to know in intellectual terms what that situation was. What he has to do is to bring into consciousness the memory with all its emotional charge and work through the emotions involved until he is able to adopt a new and conscious attitude both to the past of childhood and to the present of adult life. The patient for example shows a wish to leave the room suddenly. The analyst interprets this by suggesting that the patient fears his own impulse to kill the analyst. The patient denies vehemently that he has any such impulse and perhaps a flow of highly excited free association follows. (This is what the analyst normally takes as confirming an interpretation as, if not entirely correct, at least coming near the mark.) Some time later in the analysis the patient suddenly tells the analyst that he now sees that the analyst's interpretation was correct. The analyst then suggests to the patient that his wish to kill him arose from an identification of the analyst with his father. The patient in precisely similar fashion first repudiates this and then admits it, remembering perhaps some vivid and important, but hitherto forgotten situation of childhood rage against the father. Such types of happening are common features of analytic psychotherapy. But our description of the development of the analysis is so far incomplete because it lacks any account of why the psychoanalyst offers the interpretations he does, of what it is that goes on in his mind. To consider this will be to bring out features of Freudian theory which are important for my purpose in this essay.

The analyst's first step is to identify the behaviour. He sees its unconscious motivation in the sense that he sees it as an expression of fear of what the patient may do. He sees the purpose in the act which the patient does not see. How such unconscious purposes may be ascribed has already been made clear and of this we need therefore say no more. The analyst then explains the patient's inability to recognize this by postulating a conflict between an impulse which is directed against him and an impulse to suppress the former impulse to the extent of not admitting it. He then by means of his interpretation and the patient's response to it enables these impulses to become conscious. He then performs another work of identification in understanding the parallel between the patient's adult attitude to him and his childhood attitude to his father. Finally he by another interpretation and by allowing the patient to continue his stream of associations allows the patient to remove the hindrances to recalling his lost memory of childhood. For the patient there is an alternation between identification—the recognition of what he is doing and feeling—and the transformation by association, by working through his emotional states, of his attitudes and impulses. It is this interplay between causally effective interference and the identification of motives and purposes, I would suggest, which leads to the systematic confusion that we have noted in Freud's manner of talking about the unconscious motivation. This confusion appears, contrary to what Professors S. E. Toulmin and A. G. N. Flew have claimed, both when Freud attends to particular case-histories and when he speaks more generally and theoretically. But it is a confusion rooted in the realities of the therapeutic situation.

If we distinguish motives and causes, as Freud does not, what place are we to assign to the causal explanations which Freud offers? At once we are faced with Freud's whole theoretical structure. The child in early youth exhibited some instinctual impulse which sprang from the primary processes: the result of this was parental disapprobation or some other situation of great pain: so the impulse was repressed and with it the memory of the situation: a similar situation in later life evokes an unconscious conflict: the repressed idea with its charge of feeling causes a set of neurotic symptoms: to bring it to consciousness is to remove the cause of the neurosis. This, ignoring all the exchanges and transformations which are alleged to take place in the unconscious, is the skeleton of the causal story. If we are to evaluate it conceptually, we must note that it falls into three parts. There is first the claim that it is a correlation between certain types of childhood experience and certain types of adult behaviour. Psychology owes an immeasureable debt to Freud for having suggested so clearly the existence of such correlations, but there is nothing peculiarly 'Freudian' about them. Freud argues that a thrifty, somewhat ill-tempered attitude is the result in early life of the wrong sort of potting training or that adult attitudes to one's wife are in some cases correlated with childhood attitudes to one's mother. Bowlby argues that if at a certain period in early childhood a child is deprived of an adequate maternal figure it will later prove incapable of normal affection and will display delinquent traits. Correlations, real or alleged, of this kind might be multiplied indefinitely, and their being put forward is dependent on no particular background of theory. To test them is simply a matter of amassing evidence and as we have more and more reliable records of childhood upbringing for adult patients and others, so these claims will be conclusively verified or falsified and in many cases perhaps radically modified.

Secondly, there is the claim that remembering childhood situations (and abreacting or achieving catharsis in some other way of the emotions connected with them) will alter behaviour. This is an ambiguous claim because of the two senses of 'remember'. Sometimes we say 'remember' and mean 'make a memory claim'; but sometimes we mean 'make a correct memory claim'. George IV remembered in the first sense his generalship at the Battle of Waterloo; but he did not remember it in the second sense—he could not have done so, for he was not there. These two senses I shall call the strong and the weak senses of 'remember'. Freud moves between them. Or rather he does not attach sufficient importance to the distinction. The reason why he does not do so is bound up with one of his most outstanding empirical discoveries, that of the importance of phantasy. In some of his very early therapeutic work Freud was appalled to discover the high incidence of sexual assaults on girls by older men, for his women patients produced a number of stories of such assaults. On investigation these stories proved to be false. The patients were not consciously dishonest. But what had been traumatic had not been an actual assault but a situation in which the patient had had an infantile phantasy, in which such an assault was imagined. One of the sequels both in Freud's later work and in that of his successors to this discovery of the power of phantasies has been a neglect of any attempt to secure independent confirmation of what the patient remembers—in the weak sense of 'remember'—on the couch. There is obviously abundant evidence of the Freudian claim, if 'remember' is interpreted in a weak sense, to be found in psychoanalytic experience. If 'remember' is interpreted in a strong sense, then the verification or falsification of the claim will be of the same kind as that appropriate to the claim discussed in the last paragraph that adult behaviour and childhood experience are correlative.

Yet these two claims omit much that Freud himself and his followers would presumably consider essential in his theoretical account. So far as theory is concerned, Freud pins everything upon a third claim, that the reason why childhood events are correlated with adult experience *and* why their recall to memory has therapeutic power is *because* memories have been repressed, have been operative in some form or other in the unconscious and have manifested themselves in overt behaviour. The concept of repression is crucial here. Clearly Freud thinks of repression as a datable event, as something that happens. 'Repression' is therefore a descriptive term. Freud in his earliest writings speaks of it as an act, something we achieve, as we may in ordinary usage be said to repress or suppress some urge; but soon he is speaking of repression as the result of interaction of the preconscious system with the unconscious. So that repression is not just as it were something that happens, but something that happens to us. Can we observe repression occurring in ourselves or others? Freud's terminology is obscure to me here, but at least it is quite clear, that if we could say, 'Here is an idea of an emotionally powerful kind being repressed in me' repression could not in fact occur. We must, so it would seem, be unaware of (whether we can say 'unconscious of' I do not venture to say) repression occurring. Repression will therefore be unobservable. We can only infer that an idea has been repressed from subsequent behaviour and feelings. Furthermore, presumably a memory can only be repressed if the patient has actually met a childhood situation from which the memory derived. So that the claim that repression has occurred is logically dependent on the claim discussed above that certain alleged childhood experiences did in fact take place. But to show that they took place is not enough to show that repression occurred, and it is difficult to see what would be enough. Yet on this hinges most of what Freud says about 'the unconscious'. The unconscious explains the continuity between infancy and adult life. It is by means of repression that memories enter the unconscious. But repression is singularly elusive—except of course descriptively. A man may manifest great strain or anxiety and when he finds himself able to recall a particular memory, strain and anxiety vanish. To say that he repressed the memory is both to say that he was unable to recall it and that this inability is correlated with strain and anxiety. But if we used 'repression' thus we should merely be describing the phenomena which in Freud's use of the word the term is invoked in order to explain.

This difficulty over 'repression' extends for the reasons I have suggested to 'the unconscious'. The issue about 'the unconscious' can now be restated. Either the unconscious is an inaccessible realm of inaccessible entities existing in its own right or it is a theoretical and unobservable entity introduced to explain and relate a number of otherwise inexplicable phenomena. If it is the first, then being a real existent it requires evidence for its existence to be credible. But *ex-hypothesi* it cannot be observed and so we cannot possibly have evidence of its existence. If we dismiss this alternative as too naïve, although Freud's talk of the unconscious as the ding-an-sich behind the sense-data is naïve in just this way (it compares oddly with his other metaphor of the unconscious as the submerged part of the iceberg), then the other alternative demands that we inquire what precise explanatory role the concept of the unconscious plays. And here I find myself at a loss. For while Freud illuminatingly describes a good deal of behaviour as unconsciously motivated, and describes too how the recall of events and situations of which we had become unconscious may have a therapeutic role, he wishes to justify not just the adverb or the adjective but also the substantive form: the unconscious. Yet from the supposition of such an entity what consequences flow that could not otherwise be predicted? Freud's hypotheses as to the infantile origin of adult traits and disorders

F

can all be formulated without reference to it; indeed if to formulate them with reference to it involves reference to repression, where 'repression' signifies an inaccessible process or event (which, as we shall see, is not always the case), then the empirical scope of Freud's hypotheses is made less rather than clarified by introducing the concept of 'the unconscious'.

My thesis then is that in so far as Freud uses the concept of the unconscious as an explanatory concept, he fails, if not to justify it, at least to make clear its justification. He gives us causal explanations, certainly; but these can and apparently must stand or fall on their own feet without reference to it. He has a legitimate concept of unconscious mental activity, certainly; but this he uses to describe behaviour, not to explain it. This thesis, that Freud's genius is notable in his descriptive work is not of course original. G. E. Moore has told us how Wittgenstein advanced it in his lectures in 1931–3. But it is important to understand how much of Freud's work it affects. Before pursuing this, however, it is worth noting a possible explanation, not perhaps of why Freud attempted to use 'the unconscious' in the way that he does, but of why so many have taken it for a possible concept.

Freud picks out a whole range of neurotic reactions to particular types of situation. Examples are projection, where what the patient does not recognize in himself he nonetheless sees in others; and introjection, where an attitude of the patient towards someone else goes unrecognized and is converted into an attitude to oneself. Thus the paranoid who does not recognize his own homosexual tendencies believes that others are accusing him of such tendencies; the depressive who resented another to the point of wishing to destroy him does not recognize his resentment and transfers it to himself. Freud not only describes these conditions, he assigns to them antecedent causal determinants. Now what is done by paranoids and melancholiacs is not done consciously; and they are unable by ordinary means to become conscious of what they do. But something is done. So one might slip into saying that something happens unconsciously, not in the conscious life of the neurotic but in his unconscious life. And to fall into this way of talking is half-way to reduplicating the Cartesian substantial conscious mind by a substantial unconscious mind. The unconscious is the ghost of the Cartesian consciousness.

To return to Freud's positive descriptive achievement. Freud, of course, seeks to account not only for neurotic symptoms, but for dreams, slips of the tongue, jokes and the like. Here again it was Wittgenstein who pointed out that what Freud had done was to give not an explanation, but a 'wonderful representation' of the facts. 'It is all excellent similes, e.g. the comparison of a dream to a rebus.' When Freud 'explains' a dream, what he does essentially is to decode it. Seeing that something hidden is said in the dream is like seeing the hidden shape in a rebus or puzzle-picture. Freud saw what he was doing here with perfect clarity, sometimes but at other times he confused it with giving the cause of the dream. A dream is like those puzzling pieces of intentional behaviour the purpose of which we do not and cannot consciously avow. We betray in a dream (or in a slip of the tongue) two conflicting but unrecognized, intentions, one of which is the intention of suppressing or concealing the other. But this does not produce a resultant phenomenon from which as it were the clash of forces can be calculated: it produces a palimpsest which can be deciphered. When the patient comes to agree with the interpretation of his dream he does not confirm a causal explanation, but he supplies a missing avowal of intention. So that when Freud interprets a dream, he identifies intentions by looking at the dream in a new way: he does not guess as to an unconscious activity which is the cause of the dream.

Indeed when Freud characterizes his hypothetical explanatory realm of the unconscious, he is correctly describing dreams and experiences of schizophrenia. Timelessness, reconciliation of incompatibles, carelessness of contradiction: these terms describe the world of dream, and not the inaccessible and the unknowable. When Freud says that primary processes are ones in which the wish seeks the direct path to satisfaction, it is the instinctual attempt at satisfaction of the infant that is correctly—and perhaps not so correctly—described. Infantile sexuality is itself in part an empirical discovery of the zones in the body in which the infant finds pleasure and in part a brilliant analogy between that pleasure and the satisfactions of mature sexuality.

At this point, not very appositely, we must return to a topic touched on earlier, simply in order to make the argument more complete. In arguing that an intention was always something that could in certain circumstances be avowed, I left on one side a group of examples which are often displayed by those who wish to equate an intention with a pattern of behaviour *simpliciter*. These examples are such things as works of art and pieces of writing. When we try to elucidate what the author meant, we seek his meaning in his text, not in his mental state. What is more his avowals are irrelevant once we have the work. (Mr. T. S. Eliot is reported on more than one occasion to have said that he was in no better position than anyone else for knowing what a work of his meant.) But the reason why these cases do not make against the view that possibility of avowal is a necessary constituent of intention (or, to speak in a more precise mode, that by 'intention' we mean in part 'what the agent would say') is that in them we are not concerned with intentions in this sense at all. What Plato intended to show by argument in the *Parmenides* is one thing; what the point of the arguments that he manages to state is another. The point of a piece of writing or a work of art is to be distinguished from its author's intentions. So that to examine these examples closely is simply to come to see that they are irrelevant. But they may cause difficulty in the case of the discussion of unconscious intentions because Freud is at times among those who signally fail to distinguish between the point of a work and the intentions of its author. So are most of those who have imagined that psychoanalytic remarks about art could contribute to aesthetic understanding. But there is one exception to be made here. Just because Freud was decoding rather than explaining, where art and dreams are concerned, so he can sometimes, having an eye for what few people, at least few pre-Freudian people, had an eye for, both in dreams and in human conduct, see something in the picture, read something in the work which we might otherwise have missed. So, to use an example which comes from one of Freud's letters quoted by Theodor Reik, his analysis of Dostoievski's limitations as a novelist is not just psycho-analysis, it is criticism. Freud elsewhere discussed Dostoievski's character, but he goes beyond this when he remarks of Dostoievski that 'his insight was entirely restricted to the workings of the abnormal psyche. Consider his astounding helplessness before the phenomenon of love; he really only understands either crude, instinctive desire or masochistic submission or love from pity.' Anyone who has pondered that weakness in *The Brothers Karamazov* which springs from the failure to make the character of Alyosha convincing will feel that Freud has here put his finger on an essential limitation of Dostoievski. But because Freud is here a critic his comments stand or fall as criticism. They have no extra authority because they come from a psychoanalyst who has insight into Dostoievski's intentions and character. For the point of his novels, their merit and demerit, is independent of the author's intentions.

Finally, nothing that I have written in earlier paragraphs should be taken to mean that I consider Freud merely a naïve victim of conceptual confusion. Freud returned to the data of human behaviour so often and so thoroughly that he continally revised his theoretical concepts and went on doing this almost until the day of his death. Indeed Freud's conceptual emendations seem to me to bear out the thesis of this essay by their whole trend. Freud moves from a neurophysiological background, where 'what goes on inside' is his explanatory preoccupation, to a framework of thought in which he makes a good deal of use of the vocabulary of biological description. One example of this transformation is his treatment of anxiety which he at first accounts for in terms of sexual impulses that have failed to find an outlet. Diverted and transformed, they exert a malign influence upon the system. Conceived thus, the impulse, the sexual libido, resemble Quantity in Freud's own neurological hypothesis or the electrical impulses of the contemporary neurophysiologist. But Freud comes later on to conceive of anxiety far more in behavioural (thought not behaviourist) terms, in terms of the response of the organism to external stimuli recognized as dangerous. His concepts come to resemble those of the animal ethologists, whom indeed he influenced strongly. This systematic transformation of Freud's conception of anxiety is in

itself an epitome of the development of his thought.
More immediately relevant for our purposes is the
change in his concept of repression. When he introduces this concept at first it is in terms of lost
memory and it is, as we have seen, an essentially
explanatory concept. But we find Freud saying
later that forgetfulness in itself is not a good criterion of whether repression has or has not occurred;
and he comes more and more to use 'repression'
as almost equivalent to 'defence'. To say that something is repressed is not to draw attention now to
the pushing of a memory from one realm into
another but to some strategem whereby the personality defends itself in psychologically painful or
dangerous situations. Of course the removal of
memory from consciousness is itself such a strata-
gem but Freud seems to conceive repression more
and more in descriptive terms. So that to repress
something is to make a move unconsciously in a
particular direction and 'unconsciously' is here
used to refer to unrecognized purposes in precisely
the way which we have already elucidated. Indeed
Freud seems on occasion to narrow down his use
of 'repression' in order to refer to particular defences. (I say 'defences' rather than 'defence-
mechanisms' because this latter term begs so many
questions.) The link with loss of memory is preserved, for example, in his use of the term in connection with hysterical amnesia. But Freud ceases
to be dominated by the terminology of 'ideas'
which played such a distinctive role in the formation of the concept of the unconscious. He comes to

think of what is repressed in terms not so much of ideas as of feelings: repression consists in the inhibition of emotion. And while 'inhibition', for example, is itself a metaphor that suggests a pushing back into another realm, the use of this metaphor for descriptive purposes of this kind is common enough. If I am right, then, Freud's indispensable terms are 'unconscious' and 'repression' used descriptively; except in so far as illuminating description may count as a kind of explanation, their place as explanatory terms is highly dubious. That Freud used them in this dubious way is not surprising. All his theoretical work has a kind of creative untidiness about it. He never presents us with a finished structure but with the far more exciting prospect of working through a number of possible ways of talking and thinking. One result of this is that his conceptual errors and unclarities are usually far more interesting and suggestive than the careful precision with which so many writers on psychology equip themselves only to find that the data of human behaviour and experience are far richer than the conceptual framework into which they want to see the data forced.

CHAPTER FIVE

THEORY AND THERAPY

FREUDIAN theory was elaborated out of Freudian therapy. And in so far as the theory is a summary of clinical experience, nothing can displace it. What is more, as the theory indicates to us analogies between clinical and everyday experience, so it becomes a guide to the world of the normal as well as of the abnormal. But where Freud's high-level concepts, such as 'the unconscious', take on an explanatory role we may inquire whether they help or hinder at this point, or rather how far they help and how far they hinder. Do they in fact still reveal what goes on in the therapeutic situation or do they in some ways conceal and misrepresent it?

Consider for instance that part of therapy which consists in the recall of lost memories. The psychoanalyst hopes that his patient will come to remember his past and to see it in a new light. The theoretical assumption is that what happened in childhood can be recalled with the aid of the analyst's interpretations of symptoms, dream-material and free association. The assumption is that we have to learn the truth about early childhood if we are to be cured. But is it *the truth* that we learn in an analysis? The psychoanalyst must largely derive his assurance that it is from his trust in the concept of 'the unconscious' as the home of genuinely repressed memories. For unlike Freud in his younger days he does not normally make a thorough independent investigation of the patient's childhood, consult family papers, interview nannies, write to relatives. Certainly the psychoanalyst has something more than theory to rely on. Psychoanalysts, like personnel officers, clergymen and doctors, learn empirically what a convincing tale sounds like and come to have a good ear for deception and self-deception. But the claims of Freudian therapists go much further than any such modest empirical assurance could warrant. For they claim that what the patient imagined about his childhood at the beginning of his analysis is always less reliable than what he has remembered by the end. Suppose however a somewhat suggestible patient who knows something about psychoanalytic theory could gradually come to 'remember' a suitable childhood. The psychoanalyst would no doubt argue that such a patient could not maintain progress, and no doubt cases approximating to this example do in fact occur from time to time, and the deception is discovered by the analyst. But is the theoretical structure secure enough to guarantee that the psychoanalyst will not be deceived?

Our doubts about this trust in the theoretical structure and its keystone, the conception of 'the unconscious', may well be heightened by another consideration. It is a commonplace that psychotherapists are divided into what it is still regrettably no exaggeration to call warring factions, of which the Freudian school is only one. It might be thought that an appeal to the statistics of cure could be decisive in deciding between them. But this is not so, for all achieve roughly the same rates of cure as far as can be discerned from what is at times rather incomplete statistical information. This in itself tells one very little, for the healing of some peculiarly intractable mental disorder over a long period may produce one case history that is far more impressive in relation to the therapist's use of theory than are a number of cases of less difficult patients. All this however leaves it true that psychotherapists who advance widely different and indeed incompatible explanations of mental disorder, Freudians, neo-Freudians, Jungians, Adlerians, psychiatrists who employ physical methods and so on, all achieve cures. So that clinical success can be no test of the correctness of the theoretical explanations of the psychotherapist. Nor is it merely the differences between psychotherapists which suggest this. The clinical situation is not one in which the kind of experiment we need to test theories can easily be constructed. The experimenter wishes to devise experiments in which his hypothesis might be falsified, to elaborate situations in which his hypothesis would fail him, if it were at fault. Since he is looking for flaws in the hypothesis, it is a victory for the experimenter if he can find a situation where it will break down. The clinician wants to heal his patient's disorder in the shortest possible time. Whatever will minister to that end concerns him—and nothing else. There is no short-term coincidence between clinical and experimental aims here. This is not to say that the clinician cannot *sometimes* fruitfully experiment with his patients. It is merely to add another consideration to reinforce the view that psychotherapeutic hypotheses are not be measured by their degree of clinical success and failure. (It is a commonplace observation, anyway, that what matters most of all in psychotherapy is what sort of person you are, not what kind of theories you hold. A cynic might come to believe—wrongly, I should hold—after a little experience of psychotherapists that all that mattered for practical ends is that they should be thoroughly convinced of the truth of some theory or other, it does not matter which.)

If clinical success does not guarantee the correctness either of the explanations which the therapist used himself or of those which he gave to the patient (I am not suggesting that these will not be substantially the same), then the psychoanalyst is deprived of yet another possible source of confirmation of the patient's claims to have come to remember childhood incidents. And this strengthens the case that what the psychoanalyst is really relying on is a compound of empirical know-how and skill at detecting deception on the one hand, and a large trust in Freud's theoretical structure on the other. If my previous arguments are correct, then it is fundamentally the empirical know-how which matters. And that this would agree with what we should expect on commonsense grounds anyway is not perhaps a point against it.

The importance of all this is that while experiments may be and have been devised to test many of Freud's hypotheses in laboratory situations, those which concern repression are crucial in relation to the concept of 'the unconscious' and a necessary condition of their verification would be the occurrence of such things as the correct recall of lost memory by the patient in the clinical situation. The difficulties over verification are intensified by certain other features of Freud's theory and practice. Let us consider just three of these. First there is the fact of the patient's resistance to the psychoanalyst's interpretations. Precisely because a repressed memory is such that it has to be repressed there is a resistance to admitting it. The nearer the analyst's interpretation come to stating the truth about what is repressed, the nearer the patient will approach the situation which Freud describes by saying, 'While we are analysing the resistances, the ego—more or less of set purpose—breaks the compact upon which the analytic situation is based.' Thus failure to acknowledge the correctness of the analyst's interpretation may be due *either* to 'resistance to the discovery of resistances' *or* to the fact that the interpretation is incorrect. We envisaged earlier a situation in which the analyst's interpretations might be accepted without them being true; here we have a situation—and in this case one explicitly allowed for by Freud—when the interpretations can be rejected without being false. The fact that the analyst does use as a test the patient's reaction to the interpretation suggests that the interpretation which the analyst will stand by is the efficacious one rather than the correct one. Nothing guarantees the equation of efficacy with correctness here except the theoretical linking of repression to recovered memory *via* the concept of 'the unconscious'. And this link we have seen to be a frail one. Secondly, there is the concept of ambivalence. The interchange of love and hate is no doubt an important feature of human behaviour. But it makes the confirmation of hypotheses a more difficult task than usual if our predictions are equally verified by one and by the other. If a hypothesis on the basis of which we predict one type of behaviour is not falsified by the appearance of a quite different type of behaviour, because the types of behaviour are essentially two aspects of the same basic attitude, then clearly the hypothesis must be framed widely enough to allow for both types of behaviour, but not so widely that any behaviour whatever will turn out to be compatible with it. This is not an insuperable difficulty, but it is a difficulty which is suggested by psychoanalytic use of the concept of ambivalence.

Thirdly, the maxim that 'Every symptom is overdetermined' no doubt prevents the psychoanalyst from narrowing down his search for explanations of symptom formation too soon. But if there are always more than sufficient causes of a neurotic symptom's appearance and persistence, then the fact that a particular explanation does not produce a remedy sufficient to remove the symptom never means that the explanation was incorrect, but only that it was incomplete. So that here too there is a difficulty about the falsification of psychoanalytic hypotheses, although again not an insuperable one.

What all these considerations combine to suggest is that clinical experience could never provide adequate verification or falsification of the whole of Freudian theory. But this does not of course mean that psychoanalysts have to wait for experimental work such as that recounted by Sears and Mowrer until they can continue their therapy with confidence. What instead we are forced to conclude is that psychoanalysis as psychotherapy is relatively autonomous in relation to psychoanalytic theory. Freud's method of treatment is not altogether dependent—and this may be an understatement—on his theoretical speculation. This suggests a possible account of psychoanalysis as a therapeutic method, something as follows. The psychoanalyst's task is to help his patient to accept his present and his past. That he does not accept them as a neurotic is evident from his failure and inability to acknowledge his own purposes and motives as these are exhibited in his actions. His actions, his obsessional ritual, his hysterical blindness, are inexplicable to him as purposes because he has too narrow a picture of himself, too narrow a concept of purpose. What the concept of the unconscious does for the analyst is to provide him with a canvas large enough for any human behaviour, no matter how abnormal, to find a place in it. The description of primary processes with all their wild, untrammelled desires allows for this. By enabling the patient to bring out everything he feels and remembers, everything that comes into his mind, all the chaotic material of one life is produced and the theory (as presented *via* the analyst's interpretations) provides a framework within which it can be arranged and ordered; and labels can be found for those features of life too uncomfortable to be dwelt on hitherto. In the course of the analysis the patient has analogies suggested to him between his adult behaviour and possible childhood incidents. So his phantasies as they are brought into the light are located in terms of a childhood world of weaning and potting and parental care, of love and rage and fear. So that what the analyst provides is a way of arranging the past that is acceptable to the present. He offers not so much an explanation as an identification and then a classification. And 'the unconscious' functions here as a classificatory label, as a category into which many of those aspects of his life which are now brought to the patient's attention can be fitted.

If this is so, of course, the psychoanalyst will be strikingly independent of the theory he professes. His concepts will be necessarily flexible enough to include anything that may occur, and the 'statements' in which he expresses them will necessarily be unfalsifiable. Psychoanalysts will protest no doubt that I grossly misrepresent them; but what would they allow to overthrow their hypotheses in such a way as to lead them to fundamentally alter

G

their theoretical concepts? A number of reasons may
be adduced for suspecting that the answer is
'Nothing'. These reasons are of rather different kinds.
I will not dwell, for example, on the kind of passions
which seem to be aroused in controversies over
psychoanalysis, passions typical of controversies
about the unfalsifiable and similar to the traditional
odium theologicum. But more important than this is
the confidence which psychoanalysts have placed
and do place in parts of Freudian theory which still
await adequate experimental confirmation. They
base their confidence on clinical experience, if their
own statements are to be believed; but clinical
experience, we have already seen, will not supply
what is needed here. Furthermore, fresh discoveries
tend to be fitted into the existing framework in a
way which suggests that the framework itself could
never stand in any danger of rejection. Dr. Edward
Glover wrote very relevantly to this point when he
expressed the view that 'the basic concepts on
which psychoanalytical theory is founded can and
should be used as a discipline to control all hypothetical reconstructions of mental development and
all etiological theories that cannot be directly verified by clinical psychoanalysis. . . . It is often said
that Freud was ready to alter his formulations when
empirical necessity called for a change. But although
this was true as regards certain parts of his clinical
theory it was not in my opinion true of his fundamental concepts.' (*Basic Mental Concepts*, p. 1.)
This again suggests that the fundamental theses of
Freudian theory are unfalsifiable.

There is one other feature of Freudian theory which is relevant here. Freud attempted to construct a theory of human behaviour as such, not a theory of European or Western or, as some Marxist critics have unkindly suggested he succeeded in doing, of bourgeois Viennese behaviour. (Although sometimes to read Karl Kraus is to wonder about this.) The very fact that Freud could attempt to do this (let alone what it led him into in *Totem and Taboo*) throws a certain amount of doubt on Freudian theory in general and on the concept of 'the unconscious' in particular. For this latter concept is inexorably bound, as we have seen, to the concept of repression and what is repressed depends on which early childhood situations are painful. But this will vary according to social and family structure, presumably, and the effects of this are far from negligible, as the work of Malinowski and a great many others has shown. Freud himself does not allow for this adequately, although some Freudians have done so.

What I have argued then is not only that the concept of 'the unconscious' is difficult to make anything of in terms of the other concepts by means of which Freud seeks to elucidate it; but that it is difficult to find any place where the general structure of Freud's theory, in which it finds its place, could achieve confirmation. But the fact that clinical experience will not afford us this type of confirmation has as its corollary the fact that psychoanalysis as a method of therapy is relatively unaffected by any conceptual confusions in Freudian theory. To have argued this, however, is not to have exhausted the possible areas where the concepts of the theory impinge upon and even clash with those of the therapy.

The sharpest distinction in Freud's clinical practice is presumably that between the suffering neurotic and the successfully analysed patient. The former goes through compulsive rituals, is harassed by delusive beliefs, cannot understand his own behaviour, and cannot control it; the latter is characterized by what Freud calls 'self-knowledge and greater self-control'. Thus 'cure' for Freud means more than 'the mitigation of neurotic symptoms', which is what it tends to mean for those who apply physical methods in psychiatry. To be cured is to have become reasonable, aware of the true nature of one's situation, able to cope with it instead of being overcome by it. But curiously this whole distinction, lacking which the whole project of psychoanalysis would be meaningless, is obliterated by the determinism of Freud's general theory. It may well have been the case that it was the philosophical materialism which so influenced the scientists of his youth that first led him to assume the truth of determinism. But the whole structure of his theory leads him to see an omnipresent causation exerted upon conscious life by the unconscious. So in his mature writings he can speak both of 'the thorough-going meaningfulness and determinism of even the apparently most obscure and arbitrary mental phenomena' and of 'that greater freedom within the mind which distinguishes con-

scious mental activity—in the systematic sense—
from unconscious'. If the determinism which his
beliefs about the unconscious seem to entail is
asserted, then the difference between the obsessional
ritual of a compulsion neurosis and normal behaviour lies only in the normality of the behaviour;
for 'He could not have done other than he did' can
truly be said of the agent in both cases. Indeed there
is a sense in which the non-neurotic is more deluded
than the neurotic. For in obsessional neuroses the
patient is aware of the compulsion to perform his
ritual; whereas the normal person has the—if the
determinist is right—illusion of free decision. Thus
the psychoanalyst as therapist contrasts compulsive and unfree neurotic behaviour with normal free
choice; but as theorist his conception of unconscious causation leads him to deny this contrast by
seeing both as unfree. These are not only intoler-
able paradoxes on their own account; they make
against the whole force which the word 'compulsive' has when used of neurotic behaviour.

Nor is this the only distinction which is dis-
figured in this way. For the view of conscious mental life as the resultant of unconscious forces makes
the whole transition from neurotic to normal behaviour, the whole of psychoanalytic treatment in
other words, into a question of causing changes in
the patient's personality. Now to see psychoanalysis in this way is to lose sight of the difference
between analysis as a method of treatment and the
physical methods of treating mental disorder which
utilize drugs and surgery. Clearly these latter are

causal methods of altering behaviour. They change
the patient by changing his physiology. But in
psychoanalysis there is a large element of the treatment which consists in the patient coming to see
that certain of his beliefs are misconceptions and
that certain of his actions only make sense on
assumptions which when they are made explicit he
is prepared to reject. The patient's rationality is
brought into play. He is no longer merely an object
of causal manipulation.

This clash between the language of rationality and
responsibility and the language of determinism remains unresolved in Freud's writings. It reproduces
a philosophical crux which has an importance far
beyond the discussion of psychoanalysis, and this
is not the place to attempt its solution. But unless
we notice and indeed underline its presence, we may,
in the interests of a theoretical structure which is
infected with confusion, obliterate distinctions such
as those between the deeply neurotic patient and the
same patient after a successful analysis or between
psychoanalytic and physical methods in psychiatry.
The point is not of course that the elucidation of
these distinctions must wait upon a successful
philosophical analysis of the problems of determinism and responsibility It is rather that no treatment of those problems can be counted adequate
which does not allow their full weight to these distinctions. That they are genuine distinctions we do
not need philosophy to tell us.

It is not only that certain key distinctions may be
blurred at this point; but the whole emphasis and

direction of Freud's work may be missed. Freud is so often presented as undermining the rationalist conception of man as a self-sufficient, self-aware, self-controlled being, that we are apt to forget that although he may have abandoned such a conception as an account of what man is, he never retreated from it as an account of what man ought to be. 'Where id was, there ego shall be.' Freud's whole recognition of unconscious purposes is a discovery that men are more, and not less, rational than we thought they were. His whole method of treatment rests on an assertion that men can face and cope with their situation rationally, if only they are given the opportunity. Freud himself helps to conceal this from us by his vehement disavowal of any moralistic purpose in his work. Nonetheless he promotes a moral ideal for which rationality is central. If Freud did not believe that reasonableness is better than prejudice, the mastering of hate better than giving way to it, sympathy combined with objectivity better than blindness about the behaviour of oneself and of others, neither his theory nor his practice would have any point at all. Freud does not describe the unconscious side of our nature from any simple intellectual curiosity: he wishes us to become aware of it, to control it, to be as self-aware as possible. Mr. M. B. Foster has pointed to the analogy between the Socratic ideal of self-knowledge and the Freudian one. But if this analogy is to be pressed, an objection to it must be considered.

Throughout this essay I have urged a resemblance between the psychoanalytic use of the concept of unconscious motivation and our ordinary pre-Freudian concepts and the last paragraph may have suggested a like analogy between the method of dealing with neurotic behaviour in analytic therapy, and the kind of ascesis of appraisal which is at the heart of morality. When such analogies are drawn the response of psychoanalysts is apt to be a charge that Freud's profound originality is being missed and with it the distinctiveness of the unconscious as a system of mental events. It is the preconscious rather than the unconscious which can be thus assimilated to the normal. This charge has been levelled not only at philosophical commentators on Freudian theory and practice but at a variety of psychotherapeutic heretics and schismatics. In meeting this charge I want to make three points.

The first is that it is wrong to think of the analogy between our ordinary way of conceiving purposes and Freud's way of conceiving unconsciously motivated behaviour too simply. It is not that before Freud we were perfectly clear in our ordinary ways of talking about purpose and motive and that then Freud invented a way of talking about neurotic behaviour which at first seemed eccentric but can now be seen to resemble our ordinary pre-Freudian mode of speech. If we conceive the matter thus we do indeed underrate Freud's achievement. It is only in the light of Freud's description of the abnormal that we have acquired any adequate conception of the normal. Understanding how a purpose might be unconscious is a necessary step in understanding in anything but a fragmentary way what we mean by 'purpose' at all. So that this analogy which I have been stressing is not so much an external comment on Freud but rather an attempt to bring out what is implicit in Freud's own statement. Secondly, what I have hoped to achieve is a logical classification of Freud's uses of 'unconscious'. But I have said practically nothing about all the complex forms of behaviour which he described by using that term and whose intricate detail he so patiently mapped. Hysteria, obsessional neuroses, anxiety, paranoia—these terms are labels which tell us nothing until case history after case history has been amassed, compared, classified. And as in the descriptions so also in the actual work of therapy, it is the amassing of detail that counts. No one has grasped what is involved in psychoanalysis who does not realize the apparently endless and tortuous complexity which the process involves, the taxing of patience on the part of both patient and analyst, the stratagems and deceits, the labour and fatigue involved. In saying practically nothing of all this I have had to leave out the factual core of Freud's work. But I have tried not to forget its existence in all that I have said about his concepts. The differences between a psychoanalytic and a pre-Freudian description of our motives and development are—at the phenomenological level most certainly are—striking. But there are the resemblances also and part of my task in this essay has been to exhibit them. Thirdly, what I am arguing about the logical status of a term such as 'unconscious' has, I think, no very specific consequences for psychoanalytic theory, although it has one general implication. When, for example, Dr. Edward Glover argues against the Kleinians that they do not take seriously enough Freud's metapsychological system of the unconscious, the preconscious and the conscious, one is not to suppose that by criticising the use of the expression 'the unconscious' I am supplying materials for a defence of the Kleinian position. All that one ought to infer from what I have said is that where psychoanalytic disagreements arise it is of the first importance to formulate them as largely as possible in descriptive, empirical terms. To fly to theory too soon is always dangerous in science, but is very often a necessary danger; but, where one has a theoretical structure at once as inclusive and as flexible as Freud's is, immense care is necessary. Many psychoanalytic writers have recognized this. They see Freud's theory not as something to be accepted or rejected wholesale but to be sifted in the interests of clinical experience. All that I have tried to say is—in the interests of clarity too Freud's theory must be sifted. And the necessity of this derives from the importance of Freud's theoretical work.

If such a sifting results in the eradication of all talk of 'the' unconscious as an entity, one unnecessary source of psychotherapeutic disputation will incidentally be removed. When questions about the character of the unconscious are canvassed, for example, between Freudians and Jungians it is clear that a great many straightforward empirical and theoretical issues are bound up in the discussion. But the discussion is unnecessarily complicated by being conducted as if it were about the characteristics of an entity. Is the Unconscious only personal or also collective? Have the Jungians investigated more than the preconscious? Do they not ignore the authentic unconscious? These questions are thrown back and forth. But of course it is only possible to ask what predicates can be correctly applied to the Unconscious if we first admit that there is such an entity. Freudian writers are apt to carp at the Jungian multiplication of entities, at the contempt of Occam implied in the idea of a Collective Unconscious. But the grounds on which we ought to be dubious of speaking of the collective unconscious are ones which ought to make us dubious about speaking of the unconscious at all, except perhaps as a piece of metaphysics, an attempt at a more-than-scientific unification of concepts.

This suggestion, that in speaking of 'the' unconscious, we have left science for metaphysics is one that should not surprise us. At the beginning we saw that the attraction of the concept was that it seemed to promise a general formula by means of which a theoretical unification might be achieved in the study of human behaviour. It is now time to ask whether such a unification is in fact possible. The model for this project is drawn from physics which as the most advanced of the sciences tends also to be taken as the type to which others should approximate. To explain what human beings are and do in terms of a general theory is no doubt in some sense possible: the neurophysiologists will one day give us their full acount, which will itself be reducible to a set of chemical and finally of physical explanations. But will such an account give us what we want? It will state all the necessary conditions of human behaviour, but it will mention nothing of the specifically human. For this we need a different kind of account, the kind of portrayal that the novelist rather than the scientist gives us. In other words to portray the specifically human as human, and not as nervous system plus muscles, or as chain molecules, or as fundamental particles, is not to explain at all. Or at least it is to explain as Proust explains or as Tolstoy explains. Freud was certainly a scientist: but to remember this is to expand one's conception of science. For his chief virtue resided in his power to see and to write so that we can see too. Or can we? He sowed also this doubt in our minds.

The presentation of Freud's work as a total system leaves his writings on unconscious motivation as a matrix in which very different elements can be discerned and separated out. There is the impulse to improve upon neurophysiological explanation which leaves its mark in a presentation of the unconscious that is expressed too much in causal terms. There is the ideal of conscious rationality which lends to Freud's writings both moral ferment and prescriptive flavour. There is the recognition of what was hitherto unnoticed or if noticed turned away from. There is the construction of hypotheses about the infantile causation of adult behaviour. To attempt to separate out these elements is to learn how much Freud has to teach.

INDEX